PERIOD DECORATING

PERIOD DECORATING

Mary Gilliatt

with Elizabeth Wilhide

CONRAN OCTOPUS

First published in 1990 by Conran Octopus Limited,
37 Shelton Street, London WC2H 9HN
This paperback edition printed in 1992
Reprinted 1994 , 1995

Historical Introductions Copyright © Mary Gilliatt 1990
Creating the Style projects Copyright © Conran Octopus 1990

All rights reserved. No part of this book may be reproduced, stored in a
retrieval system, or transmitted in any form or by any means,
electronic, electrostatic, magnetic tape, mechanical, photocopying,
recording or otherwise, without the prior permission of the publisher.

British Library Cataloguing in Publication Data
Gilliatt, Mary
   Mary Gilliatts period decorating: architectural
   detail, lighting, fabric and wallpapers.
   1. Residences. Interior Design
   1. Title   747

   ISBN 1 85029 833 5

Creating the Style projects written by Elizabeth Wilhide

Project Editor Polly Powell	*Senior Art Editor* Meryl Lloyd
Consultant Editor Michael Raeburn	*Art Editors* Alison Shackleton
Copy Editor Paul Barnett	and Ruth Prentice
Assistant Editor Jane Harcus	*Picture Researchers* Philippa Lewis
Editorial Assistant Debora Robertson	and Jessica Walton
Glossary compiled by Sandy Shepherd	*Production* Julia Golding

Fabric and wallpaper photography styled by Claire Lloyd and
photographed by Ian Kalinowski.

Colour illustrations by Paul Bryant
Line illustrations by Vana Haggerty

The publisher would like to thank James Finlay, Tristram Holland and
Sandy Shepherd for their help in compiling this book.

Where terminology differs, the British word is followed by the
American equivalent in brackets.

Typeset by Hunters Armley Ltd.
Printed in China.

Picture credits: page 1 *A Chelsea Interior* by Robert Tait; page 2 *The Front Door* by Mary D. Elwell.

CONTENTS

INTRODUCTION

For whatever reason, and the sociologists have many, the idea – the comfort even – of the past seems never to have been more appealing. Of course, much of our creative make-up has traditionally been retrospective; even so, one of the most interesting general anomalies of the late twentieth century – the century that begat the Modern movement and the Brave New World and saw the filling of cities with towers of concrete, steel and glass and the despoliation of great tracts of countryside with ill-considered ribbon development – is the amount of restoration, remodelling, rebuilding and, for that matter, replicating or 'approximating' of old houses that is going on all over the Western World.

A highly decorative English mantelshelf of the mid-eighteenth century.

Eighteenth-century chinoiserie decoration at Tureholm, Sweden.

An inspiring colour scheme in an understated eighteenth-century house in Staunton, Virginia.

INTRODUCTION

Carefully strip off the layers of paint or paper in old houses and you may well be agreeably surprised by the colours and designs found underneath. This Georgian house in Ireland provided just such intriguing revelations.

Renovation and replication have become a huge and lucrative business for building contractors and period specialists, and the results can serve as the focus of an absorbing and usually rewarding quest for home-owners. In recent years there has been a resurgence of traditional-style craftsmen. Ornamental plasterers, moulding and architectural detail-makers, gilders, cabinet-makers, specialist painters, grainers and the rest are once more in tremendous demand. So, too, are skilled and sensitive builders and carpenters who are well versed in the appropriate materials and construction methods and have the 'feel' for old houses and old styles. And, if the cost and/or the local scarcity of such skilled craftsmen and contractors make it difficult to employ them, then it should still be perfectly possible,

to learn enough about appropriate styles, materials and methods of decoration to, at least, approximate the look yourself.

For some people, the accretions and additions of the generations to a building are part of its appeal. Others prefer to buy a house for the charm of its exterior and its setting, and modernize the inside as much as they possibly can. Deciding what to keep, what to dispose of and what to add are not just questions of sensibility and lifestyle: we have a responsibility to our heritage and to future generations that cannot be ignored. You should therefore look carefully at your home before removing or altering any of its original components. Even in a modern home it would be wrong to impose a style of decoration that was fundamentally out of context with

INTRODUCTION

Another room in the same house reveals the original terracotta paintwork on the panelling and the elaborate cornice and neatly panelled wainscoting. The fireplace and floorboards are original.

its architecture. If you examine intelligently the arrangement of rooms, the height of ceilings and the shape of windows, for example, you will inevitably be directed towards design decisions that are appropriate to your style of house.

STUDYING THE STYLES

Unless you are a specialist in the styles of decoration associated with different periods it can be confusing to distinguish between, or even to recognize, the various components that together form a particular style. Apart from the interiors depicted in early paintings (notably those from the Dutch and Flemish schools) and the domestic settings which can be glimpsed in the backgrounds of early portraits, there is very little record of what interiors were really like before the latter part of the eighteenth century. We can learn a great deal from old records and inventories; also, of course, there are rooms to be seen and studied in museums and stately homes (although these are almost always reconstructions). A further point is that the information we are able to gather is, more often than not, based on greater rather than lesser houses, because so little has been recorded about the latter. The early rooms shown in this book are grander than most people would aspire to. However, the elements of which they are composed are relevant and there are many pointers of style and decorating ideas to be gleaned from them.

The situation improves from the late eighteenth century and early nineteenth century, when painting

INTRODUCTION

Until the advent of photography, the only real records of decorating styles were either the backgrounds of paintings or the watercolours of interiors painted from the late eighteenth century onwards. This charming pair of drawing rooms was painted by the meticulous watercolourist, Mary Ellen Best, in 1844.

with watercolours became a highly fashionable pastime. A great many of these paintings document interiors and prevailing tastes, thus providing us with a clear picture of interior design. Later, the advent of photography served a similar purpose.

All of these factors concern the framework of a house, the actual fabric and architectural detail. A basic question that remains – and this applies whether the work is renovating a house from a particular recognized period or creating a period scheme in a modern room – is how to determine the relevant interior finishes. What are the most appropriate treatments for walls, floors, ceilings and windows? What furniture and accessories should you choose? Moreover, anyone attempting to reconstruct a period interior needs to think not only about the relevant historical style they want to recreate but how it can be reproduced in terms of their own domestic context, so that it complements

current trends, from furniture arrangement to lifestyle.

In the nineteenth century certain styles were reserved for particular rooms – for example, neo-Rococo was popular for bedrooms. Such rigidity, however, may not be appropriate today. It is usually best to follow or choose a style that is in keeping with the internal structure or, alternatively, one that is appropriate to the use to which the room will be put.

Given all these different factors, it is hardly surprising that there is a good deal of confusion about what defines a particular period of interior design. The purpose of this book is to obviate such confusion, but to be realistic rather than dogmatic in approach. Consequently, the photographs show not only authentic recreations but also schemes that may put over the 'feel' of a particular period. This book also gives a concise guide to the period styles you are most likely to want to reproduce. It starts with a brief general history

INTRODUCTION

The detail of these interior landscapes is exquisitely recorded. Note the red fillet under the cornice and the layers of fringing on the window curtains or draperies (above). The finely drawn wallpaper with its red borders, the simply styled curtains and the cast-iron stove (left) are all characteristic of the period.

of decoration from the Middle Ages to the late seventeenth century, describing the various roots and cross-fertilizations of the subsequent stylistic movements once communications between countries became more general. It then goes on to show in more detail the influences on and the components of particular periods between the early eighteenth century and the first half of the twentieth century. The photographs, sketches, swatches and colour palettes have been selected to demonstrate how such looks can be reproduced, edited or approximated today. These examples may be exact, carefully executed reproductions. In a few cases, however, they may be later interpretations of earlier styles, for example, a Victorian version of a Georgian interior design.

In short, this book aims to give aesthetic inspiration as well as straightforward, practical guidance to anyone interested in traditional styles.

A SYMPATHETIC APPROACH

There are, of course, several important decisions that the home-owner has to make before starting any kind of restoration or re-creation of a period interior. Quite apart from considerations of budget and lifestyle, the salient question must be exactly how far should you go in your attempts to preserve or recreate the past.

For example, once the approximate age of an old house has been determined from local records and clues, should you in renovating it be a purist and try to take the building back to its original form and detail? This approach, though overtly romantic and public-spirited, could be extremely dispiriting if you are used to the comforts of modern plumbing, lighting, heating and air-conditioning – none of which, obviously, would have been catered for in the original construction. Lovers of seventeenth-, eighteenth- and early nineteenth-century interiors are unlikely to care at all

INTRODUCTION

*Sixteenth-century murals were discovered in this room at Canons Ashby,
Northamptonshire. They are a great contrast to the panelled walls, ceiling and
fireplace which were added centuries later.*

for the sanitation of the periods in question, or for the heat-control (or lack of it). Nevertheless, had today's conveniences existed at the time the house was built, they would certainly have been incorporated. As a general rule, if you integrate modern utilities sensitively into a period scheme, your aesthetic conscience can be clear.

ASSESSING THE POSSIBILITIES

The General Analysis
- Is it possible to establish the exact date or style of your home?
- Has the house undergone any alterations which have changed its appearance? Have walls and windows been taken out? Has an extension been built?

- What were the rooms originally used for? (Look closely at their overall scale and proportion.)
- Is it feasible to impose another style on your home without destroying its character and features?
- If your home is modern, can you realistically introduce a period style?

The Practical Considerations
- How much can you afford to spend?
- In what ways will you need to adapt the style you have chosen to suit your way of life?
- What professional advice will you need and from whom? Do you need an interior designer or an architect? Could you approach a local museum or historical society for any help?
- Are there any building regulations or preservation

INTRODUCTION

*A combination of brick, stone and somewhat battered plaster in Vita
Sackville-West's study at Sissinghurst Castle, Kent. She and her husband, Harold
Nicolson, painstakingly restored the house in the first half of this century.*

orders to consider, or any grants that might encourage you to redecorate?

- What items are available to you in the way of architectural salvage, fabrics and wallpapers?

Looking for Clues

- Analyse the basic structure and the existing architectural features
- Try to establish what is missing and try to recognize what has been taken out
- Carry out some basic research: look at old documents, plans and pictures; examine similar houses inside and outside, and study period settings or museum displays; look at the furniture for decorative details
- Investigate behind the scenes: you could uncover fragments of original wallpaper and paint, reveal a

fireplace, find original floor tiles, or discover a panelled door beneath a flush one

A Practical Approach

- Blend electrical and central-heating units into the background: be particularly careful when putting bathroom and kitchen fittings into period settings
- Find the *right* fixtures and fittings – using architectural salvage as well as modern reproductions
- Use decorating techniques and materials that are in keeping with the style: know when it is reasonable to choose less expensive alternatives
- Be flexible: once you have decided the extent of your decoration, make sure you match it to your surroundings – do not attempt to recreate a grand country-house style in a modest cottage!

EARLY STYLES OF DECORATION

Linenfold panelling, typical of the sixteenth century in Britain.

The most significant factors in the history of interior decoration have always been social, political, artistic and technological, but the most important have concerned communications – or the lack of them. Some ancient civilizations attained high standards of domestic design, but their achievements were then eclipsed for centuries. For example, the Romans had comparatively sophisticated plumbing and heating systems. Bathhouses were practical and often luxurious; cooking standards were high. All of these technological achievements were forgotten for hundreds of years after the Roman Empire collapsed. It seems almost inconceivable that such comforts, once attained, could be lost with such little trace, but they were.

Renaissance-inspired carving, complete with painting and gilding.

Early tapestry-covered chairs around an oak refectory table in the old bakehouse of Beckley Park, Oxfordshire.

THE MEDIEVAL PERIOD

The internal strife – the perpetual internecine warring – that tore up early medieval Europe dictated that dwellings had to be fortified. The lowest floor of a house of any size was used for storage and to accommodate animals, and had narrow, glassless slit windows. Access to the living quarters was provided by steps leading up to the next level. The main living area was the hall, which was used for sleeping as well as for eating. Any architectural style evident was based on that of ecclesiastical buildings. Heating was from a smoky central fireplace. Lighting was usually provided by rush lights or tallow candles. Such furniture as there was – trestle-tables, benches, perhaps a chair for the lord of the manor or castle (hence the term 'chairman'), storage chests and, for sleeping, straw palliasses – was rough, simple, easy to dismantle and very portable. Both privacy and sanitation were somewhat minimal.

By the fifteenth century, as land rivalries settled and

Rufford Old Hall, Lancashire, an excellent example of a great hall, featuring a hammer-beam roof, a pierced screen wall, panelling and carved beams.

16

life became more peaceful, new buildings began to have less by way of fortification. The great hall was still the most important room and was often two storeys high with an open timber roof. Walls were brightly coloured and, for warmth, often covered in wool hangings or tapestries. At one end of the hall would be a dais for the head of the household and his family and guests to dine on, and at the other would be a gallery used for entertainers and travelling musicians.

Small windows were set into the walls on both sides of the room. At first these were covered by shutters; glass, if available at all, was used only minimally. Floors were covered with rushes which, according to contemporary accounts still extant, were the receptacle for all sorts of detritus.

As the century wore on, central hearths, their smoke escaping through a louvre set in the roof timbers, were replaced by fireplaces set into the wall; these had hoods to contain and direct the smoke up the chimney-stack, with the result that the visibility and the quality of the air in the hall improved. Another development was greater privacy, as more rooms were added on to the central hall. The first of these extra rooms to appear was the solar, or parlour (withdrawing room), which was reached by a primitive staircase from the dais end of the main hall. When glass began to get more plentiful and be of a better quality, oriel (projecting) windows were installed in the solar; these were the forerunners of bow and bay windows but, unlike the latter, oriel windows were always on an upper floor. Large wooden-framed four-poster beds, with curtains to keep out draughts and provide some privacy, and aumbries (food cupboards with pierced doors) were eventually added to the furniture inventory.

In the second half of the fifteenth century bedchambers were added; they usually opened one into another without benefit of passages. Kitchens were at first separate buildings, being kept away from the main living areas for fear of fire; later they were built to lead off from the side of the hall opposite the screen passage. Rush lights and candles had to be lit; matches had yet to be invented, so flame was provided by a tinderbox (a precious item of the household inventory).

Bathrooms, as such, were non-existent. Washing

ABOVE *An early beamed house in Normandy. Note the patterning of the beams on the façade and the blue-painted sundial, as well as the dovecot to the right of the house.*
LEFT *The deeply recessed window, and sturdy* sgabello *of an ancient Italian* palazzo.

and bathing took place either in front of the kitchen fire or in the bedchamber, to which hot water was ferried in jugs and bowls. Large manor houses and castles had garderobes for sanitation. These were like vertical passageways running up through a corner of a house. They were generally provided with little wooden seats and drained into the moat or, failing that, a cesspool below. Bedchambers could also have chamber pots.

Once beds had become something more than a straw palliasse, they gradually became the most valuable piece of furniture in the house, so that the inheritance of the bed was an important aspect of a person's will. Straw gave way to feather mattresses, supported by either boards or criss-crossed ropes, and were covered with furs. The next most valuable piece was the oak chest, used for seating as well as for storage, and decorated with carving or painting, and sometimes both together. Linenfold panelling began to be used for wainscoting and for the sides of chairs and benches.

THE RENAISSANCE IN ITALY

Quite apart from the socio-economic developments all over Europe, as countries became generally more civilized and exploration led to an expansion of foreign trade, there was the enormous and far-reaching influence of the Italian Renaissance. This began in the early fifteenth century. This century – the quattrocento, as it is called in Italian – was to Italy what the extraordinarily creative fifth century BC was to Greece or the enlightened eighteenth century was to the rest of Europe and to America. It was a time of discovery, invention and social evolution as well as of re-evaluation in the arts, architecture, sciences and humanities.

The quattrocento's comparative peace, after centuries of bitter rivalry and warring, meant that the great Italian families were able to turn their attention to domestic building instead of wanton destruction, to being patrons of the arts instead of marauding warlords. Interestingly, as more and more was discovered about the universe and its workings, so the civilized Italians of the time began to revel in the rediscovery of their classical past, notably the scale and variety of its architecture. The new buildings of the time reflected this fascination with the Classical age. The powerful contemporary princes, Lorenzo de Medici (1449–1492), who made his city, Florence, the centre of learning and patronage, or Federico da Montefeltro (1422–1482), who created a spectacular palace in Urbino (started as early as 1450), were as able as scholars as they were as soldiers and leaders. They collected antiquities with the same enthusiasm they showed in commissioning contemporary artists.

As unfortified palaces and splendid country villas sprang up around Rome and Florence and in the Veneto, near Venice, so painters, sculptors, ceramists, metalworkers and master cabinet-makers began for the first time to create items for domestic as well as for ecclesiastical settings. The building, decorating and furnishing of fine houses and the collection of sumptuous rugs, tapestries, furniture and works of art became an absorbing occupation among the rich.

The dome which Filippo Brunelleschi (1377–1446) designed for the cathedral in Florence (1420–1461) was hailed as the first great achievement of the new art to rival and even surpass ancient Roman architecture. But neither Brunelleschi nor any other architect of the period attempted to reproduce the domestic interiors of ancient Rome – for the simple reason that they had no idea what those interiors had looked like. Not until the eighteenth century, when the well preserved remains of Pompeii and Herculaneum (buried in AD 79) were excavated, did designers have the chance to look at a Roman domestic interior. Descriptions of ancient interiors were occasionally to be found in books, but usually only as incidental references – as in the works of Pliny the Elder (AD 23–79) or in the *De Architectura* of Marcus Vitruvius. This work by Vitruvius, an architect of the first century AD, outlined the ideas of earlier theorists, many of them Greek, and was popular up to about AD 400.

Brunelleschi's contrasting white or pale-blond plastered wall surfaces, with their grey stone mouldings and details, together with his application of antique motifs, such as pediments over doorways, laid the foundations for the revival of Classical architecture in Europe and America. And it was Brunelleschi who, in association with Alberti, established certain rules of perspective and proportion which even today dictate the standards by which we judge a room.

All through the period from the fifteenth to the end of the sixteenth century, when the Italian architect Andrea Palladio (1508–1580) brought the interrelationships of rooms to perfection, there was a general sense of harmony in decoration. At the end of the sixteenth century, Italians started experimenting with the various ways of extending a given space by visual means – that is, by the clever use of *trompe-l'oeil* effects in frescos, such as painted areas showing floor tiles laid out in perspective, and other decorative motifs.

FURNISHINGS OF THE SIXTEENTH CENTURY

By the sixteenth century Italy's great houses were almost a synonym for opulence, but by today's standards they were rather sparsely furnished. Alberti wrote that decoration was necessarily subservient to architecture and that he hated everything that savoured of luxury or profusion. (In addition, he placed strong emphasis on the *appropriateness* of every feature.) The spectacular decoration – such as lavish tapestries and the Turkish

The splendid Renaissance villa of Malcontenta in the Veneto, designed by Palladio. The noble proportions and sophisticated wall decorations are particularly noteworthy as they were far in advance of other developments in the rest of Europe.

LAYOUT

Whereas the medieval interior had been enlarged as the occasion dictated, with form following in the wake of function, the refined Renaissance sense of proportion dictated certain basic precepts based on idealized human proportions. These were rigorously applied to every sort of space, whatever its size – from a grand gallery to a small library.

The Renaissance Italians were far in advance of the rest of Europe in their domestic arrangements. Grand villas were divided into rooms, each of which had its own specific function. This idea may seem commonplace to us today, but in the fifteenth century it was totally unknown in most countries – England, for example. These rooms included vestibules for receiving visitors, galleries (for showing off paintings, sculptures and precious collections of coins and gems), bedchambers, antechambers, and – in the wake of the invention of printing and the advent of the circulation of books – libraries.

rugs that were imported through Venice (and used everywhere but on floors) – was applied to walls, floors and ceilings; it was intended to act as a foil for the sumptuous costumes of the day. Furniture, however, was mainly limited to *cassoni* (elaborately carved marriage chests), tables of monumental proportions, often topped with dazzlingly coloured inlaid marbles, or *pietre dure*, cupboards with doors intricately decorated with intarsia, beds with grandiose hangings, and armchairs and side-chairs which were arranged around the walls.

THE SPREAD OF RENAISSANCE IDEAS

Although the achievements of the Italian Renaissance were so greatly admired by visitors during this time, news travelled slowly. However, Italian artists and craftsmen had already begun to filter into France, starting there to lay the foundations of the Italian vision. When, after a period of unparalleled prosperity and peace, the French King Charles VIII, who came to the throne in 1483, managed to annex most of Italy, he took back with him craftsmen to practise their craft on French soil. France, however – like most of Northern Europe – had by this time become used to the Gothic style, and so found it difficult to adapt to the severe Italian sense of proportion. Not understanding the Italian unity, the French merely grafted Renaissance motifs on to late Gothic buildings, with results that were often curious. But, in about 1515, François I of France (1494–1547) managed to lure Leonardo da Vinci and some of his Italian colleagues to his castle at Amboise; later, in the 1530s, François commissioned major French Renaissance interiors at the Château de Fontainebleau with the aid of two Italian painters, Giovanni Battista Rosso (known also as Rosso Fiorentino, 1494–1540) and Francesco Primaticcio (c1504–1570). These two Italians, with the help of Flemish and native French craftsmen, managed to alter the whole course of French interior decoration and at the same time profoundly to influence that of England, Germany and Flanders. Of all the repertoire of motifs introduced by the Italians – masks, garlands, captivating putti, scrollwork, nymphs, and so on – the strapwork was the most greatly admired, and it became a standard feature in French châteaux and *hôtels particuliers,* as well as in the great English houses of the Elizabethan and Jacobean periods.

Now, too, French architects began to visit Italy and came back filled with enthusiasm and ideas for building in the Italian manner. More and more Italian architectural descriptions and pattern-books were being published. Alas, as in France, the principles of this new vision were often improperly understood by non-Italian craftsmen, who had no idea of the classical rules, so that the results were frequently a mishmash of classical motifs overlaid on other decorative themes.

This applied particularly in Elizabethan England, where a rather tardy interpretation of the Italian Renaissance emerged, based on second-hand knowledge derived from French and Flemish versions and the

ABOVE Elaborate marquetry typical of northern and central Europe.
LEFT Renaissance-style panelling and eclectic furnishings in a Normandy house.

20

various pattern-books that were then in circulation. There were two main reasons for this. The more important was the simple fact that England was a long way away from Italy. The other was Henry VIII's quarrel with the Pope and the Roman Catholic Church, which temporarily stopped the influx of Italian craftsmen over the Channel.

The sixteenth century was, nevertheless, a time of great prosperity in England. After the Dissolution of the Monasteries (authorized by Henry VIII in 1536) money which had previously been allocated to ecclesiastical building was to some extent diverted towards the construction of domestic houses – both in the city and in the country, and for the middle classes as well as for the aristocracy. This burst of wealth and energy continued into Elizabethan times and produced new ideas in terms of house plans, layout of rooms and construction materials. Rich landowners who wanted to build new houses often took trips to Holland, Flanders and northern France and came back determined to build along the lines of the houses they had seen there. They often backed up their sketched plans with ideas from the various pattern-books they had acquired. It can be argued, however, that the English have nearly always been better at assimilation and reinterpretation than at straightforward creation. The main results of the imposition of the classical style – partly culled from French château architecture, partly from Flemish and Italian craftsmen – on the traditional asymmetrical gabled English manor actually resulted in a whole new architectural form of great vitality, as we can see in the numbers of fine Elizabethan houses, large and small, that are still extant all over Britain. But this had very little to do with the true Renaissance feeling.

Inside the Elizabethan house decorative plasterwork and carved-oak beams were used for ornamental ceilings, and splendid friezes were decorated with heraldic, animal and floral forms learned from the Italian master plasterers – who were by now once again being allowed into the country. Walls were still decorated with hangings, tapestries, embossed leather, paintings and wallpapers (now making their first appearance). But the characteristic wall treatment of the period was wood-panelling (wainscoting). The linenfold panelling of the early sixteenth century had given way to panels which were either elaborately carved or inlaid with different woods – often with Flemish Renaissance motifs.

In Europe as well as in England windows increased in size as glass increased in quality and availability. Individual panes were still small, however; they were often diamond-shaped and framed in lead. Turkish and Oriental rugs were imported in quantities into countries such as Italy, Holland and England, where they were used mainly to drape tables or decorate walls. Rugs were brought also from Spain, a country which had produced them from the early Middle Ages. England, too, started weaving its own rugs and making needlework carpets using wool on canvas. The less well off started using woven rush matting instead of the insanitary loose rushes of the Middle Ages.

The fireplace remained the focal point of the room, increasingly for its decoration as much as for its warmth. Gothic-inspired in the Tudor period, it now became a two-storey affair in grand Elizabethan houses, with carved columns, caryatids or both; typical of the Elizabethan interpretation of Renaissance art, Classical ingredients were used as decorative motifs rather than for support.

LAYOUT

In England, as in the rest of Europe, there was a move towards greater privacy through the creation of more and smaller rooms, each of which had its own specific function. The all-purpose hall slowly evolved into a smaller entrance/staircase hall, and the *galleria* of Italian houses developed into the Elizabethan long gallery. This gallery, used for exercise, conversation and for showing off treasures, was included in most houses of any size built between about 1560 and 1650. In grand houses staircase design became more sophisticated, progressing from the heavily carved Elizabethan dog-leg stair to the rather imposing open-wall variety.

THE AGE OF BAROQUE

The seventeenth century witnessed the Baroque, and was a period during which the direction of interior design and furnishing changed completely. (The word 'Baroque' is thought, somewhat slightingly, to derive from the Portuguese *barocco,* meaning an imperfect pearl.) Italy became divided and overrun so that, by the end of the century, the baton of 'arbiter of international taste' had passed to France, the country which was to remain the prevailing influence on interior design for the next three hundred years.

Before the start of the century, the idea that a room should be *comfortable* had never been paramount. In early medieval times, people who could afford furnishings were often too busy protecting their households from marauders, or moving from property to property, to think much about 'relaxation'. During the Italian Renaissance, architects were generally less concerned with ergonomics than with ensuring that furniture fitted into the overall concept of their classically ordered and magnificently decorated rooms.

In the early part of the seventeenth century, however, decorating, furnishing and entertaining became an absolute passion for rich Italians. The country was in economic decline after the prosperity of the Renaissance years and was constantly being attacked by foreign neighbours, yet Rome in particular enjoyed the sort of urban energy or 'buzz' of Edwardian London, of Paris in the 1920s or New York in the 1970s and 1980s. Artists – among them Gian Lorenzo Bernini (1598–1680), Francesco Borromini (1599–1667) and Pietro Berrettini da Cortona (1596–1669) – who worked with equal facility as architects or as supervisors of the interior in general, were being given commissions on an unprecedented scale. For the whole idea of the Baroque age, characterized by a liberal use of curves within the classical framework of the Renaissance, was to fuse the arts of painting, sculpture and architecture within one sumptuous – even sensuous – creation. From the Papal Princes down, everyone of wealth was building as lavish a house as they could afford. And this lavishness spread to other cities. Palaces and villas provided exuberant backgrounds for balls, soirées and banquets, and furnishings and interior decoration became important status symbols.

The chief ingredients of the Italian Baroque interior – an extensive use of frescos for walls and ceilings, elaborately moulded ornamental stucco work, either painted or gilded, *trompe-l'oeil* or painted illusionist devices like 'easel paintings' with painted-on gold frames, 'bronze' roundels, 'stone' figures and the inevitable *faux* marbling (as well as wood) for floors – were like High Renaissance decoration, but more so. Suites of furniture were made for specific rooms, and included mirrors, elaborately carved picture frames and gilded panelling, consoles (with or without mirrors), useful side-tables, dining-tables, side-chairs, armchairs and plinths for sculpture. Starting now and continuing into the eighteenth century, Italian decorators and craftsmen travelled all over Europe – particularly to Austria, Germany and Russia – to fulfil commissions. All at once there was a shared European design vocabulary, so that by the mid-eighteenth century grand rooms showed a certain similarity whether they were in Paris, Stockholm, Madrid, Lisbon or St Petersburg.

THE ASCENDANCY OF FRANCE

In spite of all this bravura and magnificence, nothing could stop Italy's decline from its glory days. Design leadership passed to France, where its supremacy was so consolidated during the reign of Louis XIV, *le Roi Soleil,* builder of the magnificent Palace of Versailles (which became the seat of his court in 1682), that all other European monarchs thereafter turned to France for guidance in the matter of the arts. In fact, the roots of this French domination predated the influence of Louis XIV and his brilliant architects, François Mansart (1598–1666), Louis le Vau (1612–1670) and, in particular, Charles Le Brun (1619–1690), who produced the most stunning interiors at Versailles. Earlier, in 1633, Louis XIII had cleverly concentrated the decorative arts in France by founding a sort of royal co-operative, the Manufacture Royale des Meubles de la Couronne, usually known as the Manufacture des Gobelins. The purpose of this establishment was to provide furnishings for all the royal residences and to help instigate a national style. Another factor was that for the first time the rising middle classes began to use their rapidly increasing wealth and power; they, too,

THE BAROQUE STYLE

This richly decorated room in the Hôtel Marigny, Paris, is a particularly fine example of the French Baroque style. The sumptuous furnishings date from the reign of Louis XIV, towards the end of the seventeenth century.

Bureax Mazarin, named after the French minister of the same name, were introduced during this period. They were usually decorated, often with either boullework, ivory or exotic wood inlays of various colours.

Fabric was expensive during this period so silk damask was used to line the walls in only the wealthiest of homes and royal palaces.
Tapestries provided not only warmth but also decoration to grand interiors.

These square-shaped, high-backed chairs are typical of the Louis XIV period. They were often gilded and covered with tapestry, being edged with braid and tassels. Some chairs had stretchers for added strength.

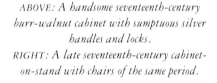

ABOVE: A handsome seventeenth-century
burr-walnut cabinet with sumptuous silver
handles and locks.
RIGHT: A late seventeenth-century cabinet-
on-stand with chairs of the same period.

now made important commissions in architecture and the arts, again with the patriotic desire to create a national French style.

Interestingly, much of the magnificence of Versailles depended to a very great extent on the careful planning of the natural lighting that fell from the many splendid windows. Sometimes the inside panes were painted with figures or portraits; sometimes they were stained, as in Holland, Flanders and England. On the ground floor, full-length 'French' windows, as they were called, have remained with us ever since. Interior shutters were particularly popular in the Low Countries.

In the latter part of the century the French influence in England became even stronger with the influx of Protestant refugees (Huguenots) fleeing the persecution of Louis XIV. Many Huguenots were skilled craftsmen: painters, gilders, carvers, silversmiths and upholsterers. They carried on much of the finest work in England at the time, causing grand English houses to achieve un-

paralleled richness. England was not the only country to benefit: 20,000 Huguenots emigrated to Prussia, many of them craftsmen who found work with Frederick I decorating the great palaces of Charlottenburg and Oranienburg. Others went to Scandinavia and to Russia. Some even found their way to America.

However, the financial cutbacks in France during the 1690s – as a result of Louis XIV's military disasters (all the spectacular silver furniture and fittings at Versailles, right down to the silver tubs for the orange trees, had to be melted down in 1692 to help raise money) – and the years of war between France and England meant that the ties between England, Holland and Italy, particularly Venice, became increasingly close. The Dutch version of Baroque became influential, as, once more, did the Italian version, as a result of the English fashion for Grand Tours – protracted cultural tours through Europe to imbibe the art of the classical Renaissance and Palladian Italy.

ENGLISH PAROCHIALISM AND EARLY AMERICAN

At this time England was once again out of the mainstream. The Baroque influence was minor and such of it as there was was sandwiched between two great classical – or, more precisely, Palladian – influences. Although the country went through more political unrest and changes at this time than most elsewhere in Europe – the unification of England and Scotland under James I; the execution of his son, Charles I, in 1649; the puritanical influence of the Commonwealth; and, from 1660 on, the splendid Restoration period of Charles II – one of the main reasons for radical changes in the practice of building had nothing to do with politics: it was the depletion of timber stocks.

At the time of the Norman invasion of 1066, England had been deeply forested. For centuries wood had been used freely to build houses and ships, to smelt iron, and for cooking and heating. But trees had never been prudently replaced. By the beginning of the seventeenth century there was a sudden and serious concern for the wood supply. Laws were passed to restrict tree-felling, so that bricks and stone began to be used much more for construction and coal began to replace wood as fuel for the fire.

In the early seventeenth century the English architect Inigo Jones (1573–1652) spent some time in Italy and France with his patron, the Second Earl of Arundel, where he made extensive and intelligent sketches of antique Roman details as well as of villas in the Veneto, designed by the great Andrea Palladio, and of the French Renaissance châteaux based on classical models. Jones was therefore the first English architect to master the classical architectural language from the original buildings; his first buildings were erected almost a century after Renaissance classical ideals had spread to France from neighbouring Italy. In spite of this tardiness the style, once started, gradually began to supersede the Elizabethan and Jacobean styles based mainly on the Flemish interpretations.

At first, though, these elegant variations on Italian Classicism – with their sophisticated French detailing – were for the royal Stuarts and for the grand aristocratic houses like Wilton, built for the Earl of Pembroke in the 1650s. Much of the rest of the country continued very plainly under Cromwell. This plain, rather

ABOVE Panelled bedroom with seventeenth-century cane-backed chairs in Westwood Manor, Wiltshire.
TOP Daneway, a romantic seventeenth-century house in the English Cotswolds.
LEFT Exquisitely inlaid walnut cabinet of the seventeenth century with stunning contemporary needlework.

utilitarian style – which was really simply a hangover from the late Middle Ages, travelled over to America with the early settlers in the first quarter of the century. Until the end of the seventeenth century, plastered and whitewashed interiors, with dashes of Dutch, German and Scandinavian influences, were to remain predominant on the East Coast and in Virginia, while Spanish Baroque would make itself felt in the Southwest.

In England, however, Charles II's return from exile – with the subsequent return of other noble exiles from scattered European courts – caused another radical change. Charles had been deeply impressed by the splendour of Louis XIV's court, and he introduced building in the new French taste. His lead was followed with gusto. Christopher Wren (1632–1723), a leading British architect, visited Paris in 1665 and came back filled with equal enthusiasm, carrying dozens of copperplate engravings of designs and amazed by the thousand or so craftsmen currently working on the Louvre Palace.

During the reign of William and Mary (1689–1702), the elaborate forms of the European Baroque evolved into the simplified, scrolling lines popular in late-seventeenth century England. Walnut was the favoured wood, and marquetry and lacquerwork were the most fashionable forms of furniture decoration.

During the early eighteenth century John Vanbrugh (1664–1726), Nicholas Hawksmoor (1661–1736) and Thomas Archer (1668–1743) produced rare (for England) great Baroque English houses; their creations were, respectively, Castle Howard and Blenheim, Easton Neston, and Chatsworth. Plasterwork, the glory of Elizabethan and Jacobean interiors, now reached new heights of sophistication thanks to superior techniques – as did wood-carving, particularly in the gifted hands of Grinling Gibbons (1648–1721), with his carved panelling, staircases, pediments and chimney-pieces.

FURNISHINGS OF THE SEVENTEENTH CENTURY

Panelling remained very popular for interiors, its sobriety relieved by the rich furniture and the new fashion for mirrors (although, at the same time, carved wooden chimney-pieces were giving way to simple marble and stone surrounds). Leather hangings were considered practical for eating areas because they did not pick up food odours to the same extent as did tapestries. In fact, towards the end of the century, tapestries were by and large being discarded in favour of

An amalgamation of early styles is shown in this dining room in Sheldon Manor, Wiltshire. The low-beamed ceiling is combined with linenfold panelling, a stone fireplace and a splendid set of caned chairs. Elegant candlesticks on a highly polished refectory table are beautifully set off by a collection of decorative blue-and-white ware.

LAYOUT
Windows were
improving all the time,
and bedrooms now
started to be built off
corridors or staircase
landings rather than
leading one from another,
with the result that
privacy was considerably
improved. Stately houses
were still showpieces for
entertaining, but they
were now becoming also
homes for people to live
in and layouts reflected
this new informality.

*Window glass appears in this
mid-seventeenth-century
painting of an interior by the
Dutch artist, Pieter de Hooch.*

wall and ceiling painting. Also, some Oriental wallpapers, panels and screens were beginning to be imported through the East India Company, as were brilliantly coloured silks.

Grand Baroque furniture was sometimes silvered or inlaid with silver; alternatively, it might be made with a variety of different woods, and tortoiseshell was fashionable. At the same time, furniture became more delicate, with legs turned in bobbin, vase, columnar or spiral twists. In fact, during this period furniture became considerably more comfortable: chairs were upholstered and edged with tassels and fringes, while chests-on-stands, chests-of-drawers, bookcases and other storage pieces were introduced, as were card- and tea-tables, in response to the fashion for drinking tea.

Although the early part of the seventeenth century featured heavy velvet for curtains, the century ended with elegant silk festoons which could be drawn up and down, and, when more warmth was required, cheaper, woven fabrics were used for curtains. Also there were painted blinds (shades) made of silk or linen.

Parquet flooring came into vogue at this time. In France it was arranged in lozenge shapes. In Germany, Scandinavia and Russia, inlaid wood floors of great richness were popular but, very oddly, they were generally covered in straw for protection.

THE GLORIOUS
EIGHTEENTH CENTURY

*Painted and gilded
Rococo woodwork of the
eighteenth century.*

The two dominant movements during the eighteenth century were the Rococo, whose lightness, elegance and informality swept most of Europe, and English Palladianism, succinctly described by the architectural critic, Sir John Summerson, as 'that balanced combination of the useful and the beautiful, of prosperity and good breeding'. The Rococo style crystallized in France and blossomed during the reign of Louis XV. English Palladianism was passed on to America, largely through the circulation of much-prized European pattern books, where it became a great influence on developing regional styles. Coincidentally, these two great movements existed and declined almost exactly in parallel with each other.

*Decorative tie-back and
silk curtain against
wooden shutters.*

*The severity of this Palladian marble fire-surround (c. 1745) is
softened by the 'informal' Rococo treatment of the mirror and
candelabras.*

29

THE AGE OF ROCOCO

The last years of Louis XIV's long reign – he died in 1715 – were a sombre sunset for *le Roi Soleil*. Financial worries and the deaths of important members of the royal family, including his son and heir, made Versailles a gloomy place, and much of the court drifted away to the lighter pleasures to be found in the circles of the duchesse de Maine and Louis's nephew, the duc d'Orléans. The grand and oppressively formal atmosphere of the court gave way to a new desire for informality, intimacy, comfort and elegance, and the most popular motifs of the period – as depicted in the paintings of Antoine Watteau (1684–1721) – concerned pleasurable diversions such as hunting, lovemaking and the simple joys of rurality. To these were added the wonderful fantasies of chinoiserie and *Turquerie,* born from the opening up of trade with the Far and Middle East.

Comfort and convenience, rather than display and ceremony, were the leitmotivs of this age which immediately preceded the Rococo period – an age described by the art historian Charles McCorquodale as 'the last wholly original expression of the aristocratic ideal in European art'.

Although the name Rococo is thought to have come from *rocaille* – which refers to a specific type of decoration derived from shell-work in grottoes – the Rococo movement was distinguished essentially from the heavy and disciplined grandeur of the Baroque by its free asymmetry, its obsession with light, its fantasy, its gossamer-fine carved plasterwork and ornament which invaded, if allowed, every surface.

The first real phase of the Rococo occurred in France; from there it spread all over mainland Europe. It came about after the death of Louis XIV, in the handsome period known as *La Régence* (1715–1723), when the duc d'Orléans acted as regent for Louis XV. The Regent was a great connoisseur of architecture, decoration and the arts in general, and for most of his regency he kept his seat of government and court in the Palais Royal, Paris. Although in 1722 the court finally moved back to Versailles, Paris remained the artistic leader of Europe until the end of the eighteenth century – and, indeed, intermittently up until the end of the first quarter of the twentieth century.

THE ROCOCO STYLE

This room in the Grand Hôtel Faligan, Belgium, displays many elements characteristic of the Rococo style. The room was designed and furnished largely around the middle of the eighteenth century.

Rounded corners and elaborate decorative woodwork are typical of Rococo interior decoration.

Boiserie (panelling) painted in pale colours and picked out in gilt served as a suitable backdrop for the rich furnishings of the Rococo.

Mirrors were an important element of the style as during the day they maximised light from windows and at night they reflected the soft glow of many candles.

These chairs, with their delicate frames and curving lines, are sometimes termed 'Louis-XV style' in recognition of their evolution during this period.

Gilding was a popular embellishment of furniture during the eighteenth century and complemented the increasingly sophisticated upholstery.

Here, the arrangement of furniture is decidely twentieth century. At the time, most furniture would have been pushed back against the wall.

*An authentic eighteenth-century atmosphere is successfully and luxuriously recreated
in this modern Paris apartment. The sofa and centre table are more
Neoclassical in style.*

The Rococo interior reached its apotheosis in the first half of Louis XV's reign (1715–1774). Typically it would have had rounded corners, arched doors and windows, depressed arches set into the walls, elaborately coved ceilings together with a highly ornamented frieze decorated with 'C' and 'S' shaped scrolls, shells, flowers and ribbon motifs, and fancifully outlined panelling, gilded and painted white or ivory. As a fashionable alternative, walls could be highly lac-quered, using the new method discovered by the brothers Martin (hence the name *vernis Martin*), which often produced a beautiful deep green. Mirroring was used lavishly, with mirrors set over console-tables, and large panels of mirror-glass recessed into the *boiserie* (wooden panelling) opposite tall overmantel mirrors. Sometimes entire walls and/or ceilings were lined in mirror. In summer mirrors were used to screen fire-places. Mirrors were even used as sliding window-

In his painting, Breakfast, *François Boucher successfully mirrors the changing mood of the mid-eighteenth century. While the room is still grand, the dainty tea-table set for a cosy breakfast reflects the growing desire at the time for more intimate and informal rooms.*

shutters which, cunningly disguised in the panelling by day, completely disguised the windows at night. Elaborate hanging mirrors contributed to the scene of endless reflections. A great number of candles were used. Normally these were held in branched candelabra made of crystal (to help reflection) and hung low in the centre of the room; alternatively they could be mounted in candlesticks set in mirrors (*girandoles*) or set close to walls or mirrors, further to reflect the light and to draw attention to the elaborate mouldings.

FURNISHINGS OF THE ROCOCO

Furniture was light, often gilded, with gracefully curved legs. Very often, sets of furniture would be made especially for a room. In fact, the best interiors of the Rococo period achieved a light-hearted but splendid synthesis between fixed and movable decoration and furniture. The comfortable, curvaceous 'Louis Quinze' *fauteuils* (armchairs), with their accommodating shape and well-rounded padding on the seat, back and arms,

were – and still are – some of the most agreeable seating ever devised, fundamentally pleasing to both the eye and the human frame.

Fabrics followed the graceful and ornamental feel of the wall decorations. Until about 1730, the coverings on grand chairs and on chairs in the best rooms were in two parts and detachable, made to slip over the backs and the seats and to fasten either with hooks and eyes or with eyeletted tabs that hooked on to studs fixed under the seat rail. These covers could be removed when the house was empty or, presumably, just for cleaning.

After this period loose covers were routinely placed as protection over precious upholstery. The practice was particularly important because at the time fabric was available only in narrow widths, which had to be seamed together; the covering was therefore weaker than if it had been made from a single unit of fabric.

Carpets graduated from table covers to floor coverings; those made in the royal factory of the Savonnerie, as well as the tapestry-weave carpets from Aubusson, became as popular as Oriental rugs. They were typically to be found laid on magnificent parquet floors. People still placed chairs, rather than bedside tables, by their beds, but the commode (chest-of-drawers) very conveniently replaced the old traditional lift-up-lid chest.

Wallpapers started to become increasingly popular, particularly for lesser rooms. Madame de Pompadour, that renowned leader of fashion, had 'English' paper (as flock papers were called) in her luxurious bathroom/dressing-room at the Château de Chimys in the late 1750s. At that time wallpaper came in sheets rather than in rolls. From 1720 onwards, hand-painted papers with images of branches and birds, sometimes with human figures in a landscape, were imported from China. Tapestries were still very popular for bedrooms, although they sometimes gave way to velvet hangings in winter and taffetas in summer; Chinese printed silk taffetas, known as 'Pekins', were the most highly prized. All such wall-hangings were usually nailed to battens fixed to the wall, and the nails were masked by some kind of border, or 'fillet', of carved or gilded wood. The most usual window treatments were 'pull-up' curtains like Austrian blinds (shades).

THE SPREAD OF ROCOCO

All this French sweetness and light was, thanks to pattern-books, engravings and peripatetic craftsmen, diligently copied in Italy, Spain, Austria, Hungary, Poland, Bohemia and Russia, but most of all in Germany. In Germany, still divided into independent states or principalities, the Rococo reached a particularly rich expressiveness, mostly because of the intense rivalry between the various princes, each of whom tried to surround himself with more opulence than the next. The abundance and gaiety of the German Rococo culminated in Bavaria with the exquisite Amalienburg hunting lodge in the grounds of the Nymphenburg Palace, and in Frederick the Great's various palaces around Berlin. Also outstanding in Germany at the time were the great porcelain factories of both Meissen and Nymphenburg.

The Rococo was introduced to the royal Scandinavian courts in the 1730's and 1740's. The leading architects and designers had trained in Paris and brought their sophisticated designs back with them. Rococo ornament became a popular feature of bourgeois interiors much later in the century.

Obviously, such complications in decoration required immense skill and control. In less experienced hands it became over-effusive and vulgar; in his treatise, *De la distribution des maisons de plaisance* (1737), the architect and critic, Jacques-François Blondel lamented with feeling the positive 'jumble of shells, dragons, reeds, palm-trees and plants which is the sum total of decoration nowadays'.

Although the Rococo period in mainland Europe lingered well into the 1770s — Voltaire, in his *Temple of Taste* (1773), wrote of 'everything panelled, varnished, whitened, gilded and straightaway admired by gapers' — in fashionable Parisian circles it had already started to wane in popularity by the 1740s. In 1756 the Marquis de Marigny, the Minister of Arts (who happened to be the younger brother of Louis XV's mistress, the influential Madame de Pompadour), suggested that competitions should be held 'in the interior decoration of grand residences, in order to correct the poor taste in ornamental design which prevails today'. Yet another new style was emerging, this time influenced to some extent by the British.

ABOVE *Ornate German Rococo in Potsdam.*
TOP *An Italian late Rococo bureau.*

*The 'China-kitchen' of Tureholm, Sweden, is a good example of the charming paint
effects achieved in Scandinavia during the eighteenth century.*

ENGLISH PALLADIANISM

Britain was the sole country in Europe in which the Rococo had comparatively little influence. During the reign of Queen Anne (1702–14), furniture and interiors had continued the William and Mary tendency to get much lighter and more delicate. The so-called 'Age of Walnut' was at its zenith at this time and an enormous number of new types of furniture were designed. Mostly with cabriole legs and claw- and/or paw-feet, these included chests of drawers, lowboys, highboys, day-beds, games-tables, card-tables, side-tables, comfortable chairs of all sorts, and the first tables made especially for the dining-room (as opposed to the collapsible tables, which could be moved around so that people could eat in whichever room happened to catch their fancy). As in France, series of beautiful mirrors completed the scene.

But in 1715 the Earl of Burlington (1695–1753), a highly respected amateur architect, on his return from extensive travels in Italy, brought with him a very splendid collection of original drawings by Andrea Palladio, and these he proceeded to reproduce and circulate. In the late 1720s and early 1730s some very faithful copies of villas originally designed for the sun-baked Italian Veneto were somewhat inappropriately built in the damply grey English countryside – 'perfectly contrived for the coolness agreeable in Italy but killing in the North of England', as Lady Mary Wortley Montague wrote to a friend in 1753.

The style did not remain pure for long. The underpinnings of the previously admired French and Franco-Dutch Baroque were amalgamated with Palladianism (the emphasis being on the classical), so that another regurgitated and uniquely British style evolved; this style went on to set the pattern for both grand and smaller houses not just in Britain but in the new colonies of North America, for news was now beginning to travel quickly: 'There is no fashion in London,' wrote a commentator in 1720, 'but in three or four months is to be seen in Boston.'

Burlington, Colen Campbell (1676–1729), William Kent (1684–1748), John Wood (c1705–1754) and other architects built and decorated some of the most beautiful houses and interiors in Europe. Burlington's villa at Chiswick (now known as Chiswick

ABOVE A watercolour by A. Sebriako of Ditchley Park, Oxfordshire.
LEFT A symmetrical façade in Ely, England.
TOP A watercolour showing Palladian room arrangement.

House), with an interior largely designed by William Kent, was based on Palladio's Villa Rotunda near Vicenza, as was Mereworth Castle in Kent. Houghton, built in Norfolk for Sir Robert Walpole, again with interiors by Kent, was another outstanding house. Holkham Hall, also in Norfolk, had a spectacular entrance hall modelled on a Roman basilica with details derived from both Palladio and Vitruvius.

Since the illustrations by Palladio failed to include any ideas for furniture, William Kent had to produce designs which he and Lord Burlington deemed appropriate for what were essentially sixteenth-century

The drawing room at Peckover House, an early Georgian building in Wisbech, Cambridgeshire. The Rococo influence is evident in the elaborate plasterwork around the mirror and, to some extent, in the Chinese-Chippendale-style side-tables.

Italian interiors. Although Kent had spent very little time in Venice and Vicenza, he had spent several years in Rome and Florence, so he turned for his inspiration to these two cities as well as to the architecture of Inigo Jones. At the same time he imbued his designs with his own vigorous interpretation, appropriate to the time. His massive and somewhat architectural pieces influenced both English and American furniture for some years. Again, his concepts were printed and distributed in books that were extremely useful to designers and craftsmen on both sides of the Atlantic.

A typical Palladian interior would have dark silk- or velvet-hung walls studded with paintings and articulated by very architectural door cases and window frames topped by massive ceiling cornices (crown molding) and coved ceilings. Woodwork was usually painted a pale colour, with details picked out in gold. In some rooms tapestries on the walls offset dark wooden floors, and doors were set against brilliant white-and-gold plaster-work and large painted ceiling roundels. Just as the French Rococo brilliantly reflected the sophistication of Parisian life, English Palladianism was perfectly suited to the grand houses of the more sober English aristocracy.

EARLY CLASSICISM IN EUROPE

In the mid-1750s the archaeological excavations of Pompeii and Herculaneum, with their astonishing discoveries of entire houses and villas that still retained their interior decoration intact, gave a fillip to the study and understanding of classical buildings. The interest in Classicism was further enlivened by a scholarly controversy about Greek supremacy over the Romans.

Le goût grec – 'Greek taste' – was the term used in France to describe the nation's Classical buildings and interiors. Thick garlands, fluted straight surfaces and ribbon decoration were introduced to interior furnishings. One of the first architects to practise the style, Louis Joseph Le Lorrain (1715–1759), provided drawings for a dining-room in a grand Swedish country house called Åkerö (1754), owned by Count Carl Gustav Tessin. It was much admired, and Count Tessin, a respected arbiter of taste, brought the style to Scandinavia as a whole; here, as in Russia, the new style caught hold some time before it spread to the rest of mainland Europe.

Jacques Ange Gabriel (1698–1782), Louis XV's court architect from 1741, who designed the Place de la Concorde (then Place Louis XV) and the École Militaire in Paris, was also the architect of that perfect little Classical building, the Petit Trianon, commissioned for Madame de Pompadour. All the major rooms, notably smaller than normal, were rectangular and decorated in soft tones of grey, white and pastels. Gabriel produced also a series of *petits appartements* for Louis XV at Versailles; these elegantly small rooms, designed for greater comfort and intimacy, had restrained door cases, cornices and wall-panels, painted white and grey or pale green, and fine marble fireplaces surmounted by large simple mirrors. These *petits appartements* started the fashion for smaller rooms which, together with simpler furniture (with tapered fluted legs), rapidly spread to become the norm for elegant living in the reign of Louis XVI. The style subsequently became known as Louis Seize.

Although the French taste was still greatly admired by the rich and influential throughout the rest of Europe and Russia, the middle classes began to look to England for its sturdy common sense. For example, an article in a German publication, the *Journal des Luxus*

und der Moden, which started to appear in Weimar in 1786, told its readers that 'English furniture is almost without exception solid and practical; French furniture is less solid, more contrived and more ostentatious' and added that 'England will . . . maintain its position of dictating taste in this sphere for a long time to come'.

Two other fairly universal fashions of the period were the painting of rooms to make it seem as if you were out-of-doors and the use of graining, marbling and other cunning effects achieved with paint; the latter became so popular that paint effects began to supplant interior architectural features. Walls became flat with shallow chair-rails and friezes, and chimney-pieces – hitherto so important – became no more than surrounds to the aperture of the fireplace. If elaborate paintwork was too costly, use was made instead of papers printed with simulations of marbling, stucco work and other architectural features as well as complete pictorial scenes.

ABOVE *This room, with its restrained elegance, was actually designed earlier this century by the American Elsie de Wolfe, illustrating the abiding popularity of the Neoclassical style.*

OPPOSITE *A room in the French Neoclassical taste at Bagatelle, near Paris. Observe the smaller, more intimate space and the altogether simpler treatment of mouldings and furnishings.*

ENGLISH NEOCLASSICISM

By the latter half of the eighteenth century, the English aristocracy's habit of sending its scions on the Grand Tour had led to an unprecedented degree of informed patronage. Having soaked in the classical ruins of ancient Rome, the glories of Renaissance Tuscany, the wonders of Venice and of the Veneto, not to mention the Rococo of the rest of Europe, these young men returned knowing exactly what they wanted to create for themselves and had the money to employ the best architects, artists and craftsmen to see that they got it. They were also intensely interested in being at the forefront of fashion, a very eighteenth-century pre-occupation: as one style followed another, they built, altered and rebuilt houses to keep abreast of the times.

Three great architects, each well known for their interiors, dominated the early Neoclassical taste: Robert Adam (1728–1792), Henry Holland (1745–1806) and James Wyatt (1746–1813). The Palladian movement, with its base in classical antiquity, had already become popular in Britain, but these three architects now introduced elements of French Classicism to the strongly Roman antiquarian style, producing a lighter style with fewer ornaments.

Robert Adam, who spent several years in Rome, was a firm follower of Piranesi (1720–1778) – a champion of Roman architecture – and had studied under the French architect and painter Charles-Louis Clérisseau who was also in Rome at that time. After his visit to Spalato (Split), Adam produced his influential *Ruins of the Palace of the Emperor Diocletian* (1764). He returned to Britain in 1758 and set up practice with his brother, James (1730–1794).

Adam is important because he made detailed studies of classical remains (instead of looking to existing, often misleading, engravings). He used his knowledge to create a deliberately eclectic style. This style of decoration was not fundamentally architectural, but was largely a decorative style for interiors. Adam preferred unifying all his surfaces with one style of ornament. This approach enabled him to fit his interior schemes into existing shells like Syon House, Kedleston Hall and Osterley Park, which was just as well, for few large new houses were being commissioned during his time. Interestingly, Adam worked in conjunction with Chippendale on a number of projects, an early instance of furniture and interiors being considered as a whole. Although 'Adam colours' are now thought of as pastel rose, greens, blues and yellows, his early schemes were really very colourful – as were those of a contemporary, Sir William Chambers (1723–1792).

In the late 1760s, Adam and the many who emulated him were using more delicate classical motifs, working in low relief and in progressively more adventurous colours. Adam himself used gilt sparingly except in his richest interiors (for example, Syon House, done for the Duke of Northumberland). Many of his carpet designs echoed those of his ceilings. By this time English carpets – Axminsters, Wiltons and Kidderminsters – were beginning to become popular amongst those who could afford them.

Robert Adam's drawing from the 1770s for Northumberland House, London.

Adam also introduced the Etruscan style, inspired by red-and-black Greek vase decoration and having a lot of terracotta colouring. He and his brother James claimed in their *The Works in Architecture of Robert and James Adam* (1773–9) that their designs had brought about a kind of revolution. And they were right. The elegant Adam style, in both furniture and decoration, is now thought of as the epitome of late eighteenth-century taste. By 1780, however, Adam's popularity was beginning to wane. William Chambers rather insultingly called Adam's decoration 'filigrane toy-work'.

Henry Holland married the daughter of the great landscape architect, Capability Brown (1716–1783). Holland had a thorough knowledge of the new Louis Seize style plus a good French first assistant, J P T Trécourt. Best of all, he had good connections with the Whig aristocracy and received commissions from the kind of clients best able to perpetuate – and pay for –

some elaborate but nicely idiosyncratic Gallic interiors. One such client was the Prince of Wales (later George IV), who gave him the plum job of reconstructing his London residence, Carlton House. The interiors were by all accounts beautiful but are sadly no longer extant. There are illustrations of the splendid Chinese Room (something of a departure for Holland) in Thomas Sheraton's *Cabinet-Maker's and Upholsterer's Drawing Book* (1791–4) and in William Pyne's *Royal Residences* (1829). Sheraton's book was read all over Europe and America and was enormously important in spreading the English version of Parisian taste. Holland's attention to detail was legendary, and he was admired as much for his thoughtfully heated window-seats as for devices like gilded pelmet boxes with eagles supporting draperies – the eagle becoming a leitmotiv in French, English, German, Austrian, Russian and American designs at the turn of the century.

James Wyatt was something of an anomaly. He returned from his Italian studies a dedicated classicist with a great love of Palladio and Raphael and convinced that Adam had corrupted the pure classical taste. Yet he produced two great neo-Gothic houses, Ashridge in Hertfordshire and Fonthill Abbey in Wiltshire. His view of the increasing eclecticism of the 1770s was that 'Grecian must be Grecian – but fancies such as Gothic, Moorish, Chinese, etc., might be imitated – some of them capable of being reduced to rules'. And, indeed, he could turn his hand to anything including revived Baroque for Windsor Castle. He was considered to be the *enfant terrible* of the time and to have ruined a brilliant career through debauchery and irresponsibility; Catherine the Great of Russia, who had considered commissioning him, suddenly dropped him. Nevertheless, he created some of the most exquisite interiors of the age, including the serenely classical Heveningham Hall in Suffolk, which would be monument enough to any career.

Fashionable styles filtered down through all levels of wealthy society. By this time the middle classes were sufficiently prosperous and discerning to be able to commission local builders who carefully followed the designs for windows, doorways, chimney-pieces and staircases as shown in architectural handbooks of the day. The results were countless exquisite small houses, which can still be seen in cities, towns and villages all over the country.

GOTHICK AND CHINOISERIE

Although contact with the Rococo style in Britain came mainly through furniture (Thomas Chippendale, for example, produced a delightful series of designs), actual Rococo decoration being rare, there were two interesting offshoots of the fanciful look which resulted in some particularly charming English interior styles: the Gothick (with a 'k') and chinoiserie.

The contents of Batty Langley's *Gothic Architecture* (1747) caught many people's fancy. In this book a wide variety of medieval sources had been plundered for inspiration, producing some fantastical interiors that bore as little resemblance to medieval rooms as Post-Modernist decoration does to Palladianism. Still, it

The fanciful Gothick mouldings at St Michael's Mount, Cornwall, are highlighted by the blue colour scheme.

was a highly decorative genre, culminating in Horace Walpole's house, Strawberry Hill, in Twickenham, near London. (The term 'Strawberry Hill Gothick' comes from the name of this house.) Robert Adam, James Wyatt and other architects continued to produce some Gothick-inspired interiors, and so the style remained sporadically fashionable through the second half of the century until it was superseded by the full-scale Gothic Revival of the early 1800s.

People were also much attracted to the Chinese and Japanese imports – the lacquered furniture, wallpapers (which were considered great status symbols) and porcelain. Since the originals were in somewhat short supply, imitations were produced in vast quantities. The prodigious Chippendale designed furniture and mirrors in the chinoiserie vein, and craftsmen all over the country experimented with various lacquered effects (often called 'japanning', for obvious reasons) as well as other exotic effects like tortoiseshell. Some splendid chairs, cabinets, bureau-bookcases and secretaires resulted from this interest, not just in the most usual black but in red, green, chestnut, white and, on occasion, soft blue.

41

AMERICAN STYLES

By the beginning of the eighteenth century American interiors and architecture had generally advanced enormously in sophistication by comparison with the simple and somewhat austere styles that had prevailed. During the reign of William and Mary (1689–1702) there was an assiduous search for comfort and elegance as American villages developed into towns and then into cities at an astonishing rate.

Britain's new shipping and trading links had greatly affected its colonies: the substantial increase in British exports allowed Americans (in particular) to enjoy all the everyday amenities of the mother country. Daniel Marot (1661–1752), a French Huguenot refugee brought from the Dutch court, was court designer to William and Mary, and his opulent designs, recorded in elaborate engravings, were much admired and emulated in America long after the style had gone out of fashion in Britain. The style was finally superseded by the sumptuous curves, cabriole legs, hoof-feet and Oriental contours of the Queen Anne period (1702–1714), which again lasted many years longer in America than in Britain. This was, indeed, an important period for American decorative arts, with earlier foreign and Far Eastern influences beginning to be absorbed as elements of a cohesive *American* style. The British Stalker and Parker treatise on japanning

was familiar to American craftsmen, appearing towards the end of the century in the catalogue of The Library Company of Philadelphia. Interestingly, American japanned furniture went through several stages. At first, as in England, it was a conscious imitation of Oriental decoration, then it became a humorous caricature, and finally it synthesized Chinese and European Rococo designs.

The vase-like outline of solid splats in the back of 'Queen Anne' chairs, not unlike the profiles of Oriental porcelains; the claw-and-ball feet, based on early Chinese carvings of dragons' claws clutching a pearl; the carved shells of the Rococo; the acanthus leaves of Rome and Greece, revived during the Renaissance and the English Palladian movement – all these, and other features, became regular motifs in the splendid furniture that was now being made by American craftsmen. Handsome side-chairs, tables, highboys, lowboys, bureaux and fall-front desks (to accommodate the new literacy – eighteenth-century Americans were great letter-writers) were combined with the new upholstered armchairs, couches and day-beds. These were matched by the equally handsome architectural details of the fine houses that were now increasingly common in the major seaboard cities. Sliding sashed windows, classical mouldings and details, elaborately framed and carved

ABOVE *An American chest of 1784, with a turned chair of an earlier date.*
LEFT *The vase-like splats on these Queen Anne chairs contribute to the eighteenth-century refinement of this room in Hurricane Hall, Kentucky.*
OPPOSITE: *An eighteenth-century bedroom at Kenmore, Virginia.*

doorways, beautiful wood floors and sometimes even cupolas served to emphasize the new graciousness.

Country homes, by contrast, were still built with rural simplicity and equipped with solid, rustic furniture, often painted with hearts, geometric designs, flowers, leaves and other Dutch, German and Scandinavian motifs, as well as the roses, thistles and crowns associated with the British royal coat of arms.

In fact, it would not be unfair to say that, until the end of the colonial era, in 1776, British fashion remained the arbiter of taste for most Americans. Numerous pattern-books were exported from London, pored over and used as models for somewhat sparer, more restrained and often more refined American versions. William Kent's *Designs of Inigo Jones* and William Salmon's *Palladio Londinensis*, both published in 1727, were avidly absorbed by the upwardly mobile middle classes, anxious to build their colonial mansions in the latest taste. The Thomas Hancock House, built in 1737–1740 on Beacon Hill in Boston, is a splendid example of these handsome new houses, with their meticulously kept outbuildings and the characteristic Georgian proportions of a central pediment door with balanced windows on either side. Thomas Chippendale's *Gentleman and Cabinet-maker's Director* (1754) was equally successful. The book inspired a school of

cabinet- and chair-making in Philadelphia that developed into the most sophisticated furniture-design movement of the century.

Regional styles were particularly individualistic in America because of the variety of the colonizing groups. In cosmopolitan Boston, cabinet-makers were strongly influenced by English fashions, but the results were pleasingly tempered by New England restraint. A cabinet-making dynasty comprising two Quaker families, the Townsends and the Goddards, evolved in Newport, Rhode Island, and poured forth a huge number of beautifully made pieces featuring elaborate shell carvings in native walnut and imported mahogany, with local chestnut used as a secondary wood. In Connecticut, cherrywood was used a great deal for the handsomer pieces of furniture, while New York (originally colonized by the Dutch and called New Amsterdam) remained faithful to its Dutch heritage, producing a blend of different construction techniques, first largely in walnut and then in mahogany. Further north, up the Hudson Valley, native woods like maple and ash were used for the less sophisticated furniture that commonly featured in the prosperous Dutch stone houses.

The furniture in the houses of the isolated plantations of the South was at first modest. However, we know that during the eighteenth century thirteen cabinet-makers lived and worked in Williamsburg, Virginia (almost certainly there were more), and some beautiful items were also produced in Charleston, South Carolina. America's first Palladian house was built in the 1740s on Ashley River, at Charleston, by John Drayton. Also of importance during this period was Monticello, the house Thomas Jefferson designed for himself in a Palladian style in the 1770s.

Towards the end of the 1700s, the taste for rectilinear furniture reasserted itself as people once more became interested in Classicism. Furniture-makers continued to adapt British designs, now following patterns prescribed by George Hepplewhite in *The Cabinet-maker and Upholsterer's Guide* (1788) and by Thomas Sheraton in his influential *Cabinet-maker and Upholsterer's Drawing Book* (1791–1794). The designs published by these two cabinet-makers were important influences on the Federal Style (see page 71).

ANTIQUES AND
MODERN FURNITURE IN
A GEORGIAN DRAWING-
ROOM

CHANDELIER CHAIN
DISGUISED WITH RED
SILK AND FRINGING

CURTAINS TOPPED BY A
PAGODA-STYLE PELMET

RESTRAINED
MOULDINGS ON THE
CORNICE AND
FIREPLACE

CENTRAL GILT-FRAMED
PAINTING HUNG FROM
A DECORATIVE BOW

CURTAINS HELD BACK
BY GILT ACANTHUS
LEAF EMBRASSES

TWO SMALL PAINTINGS
FLANK THE FIREPLACE

ORIENTAL RUG
PROVIDES A FITTING
FLOOR TREATMENT

SELECTION OF BRONZES
ADORN THE
MANTELSHELF

GEORGIAN

CREATING THE STYLE

Stylistically, the Georgian era really covers the period from the accession of King George I to the British throne, in 1714, to the end of the 1780s. The early Georgian era was dominated by Palladianism, a style based on the classical purity of Andrea Palladio's sixteenth-century Italian villas. Many large houses, based heavily on Palladio's designs, sprang up throughout Britain, a notable example being Chiswick House, the villa Lord Burlington had built for himself, with interiors by William Kent. The mid-Georgian period was distinguished by a flirtation with the Gothick (with a 'k'); a penchant for chinoiserie, following the opening up of trade with the Far East; and a belated fashion for the light-hearted Rococo of Louis XV, much more popular in Europe than in Britain. The furniture designer Thomas Chippendale (1718–1779) encapsulated all of these various styles in his work. The late Georgian period, much influenced by the amazing archaeological excavations of Pompeii (from 1748) and Herculaneum (from 1709), is characterized by lighter, finer furniture and decoration.

Although fine examples of eighteenth-century furniture are both very rare and very costly, there are still some exceedingly pleasant minor pieces around. Also available, of course, are excellent reproductions, pieces of porcelain and glass, and old fabric and wallpaper designs. Certainly you can at least approximate the Georgian style in a well proportioned room.

RICH, RED SILK COVERS
THE WALLS, FINISHED
WITH A GOLD FILLET

*An authentic colour scheme in an
eighteenth-century drawing-room
in England.*

45

Culzean Castle, one of Scotland's finest Adam houses.

A beautifully restrained but comfortable late Georgian interior.

Dark green panelling, with mouldings picked out in gold.

FIREPLACES

During the Georgian period coal was an increasingly used fuel. Fires provided interiors with much of their artificial lighting and all of their heating. This practical importance of the fireplace was stressed in strong architectural terms.

Fireplaces in the Palladian style are often made of white marble and are designed to express the Classical Order – with columns supporting a lintel. Above the lintel there might be a pediment, a sculptural relief or a large, gilt-framed picture or mirror. Caryatids sometimes provide a distinctive decorative embellishment.

Elements of Rococo whimsy, Gothick or chinoiserie motifs might be included in a Georgian fireplace if these styles are expressed in the architecture. These would reflect one of the fashions current around the middle of the century.

As the century progressed, architectural details become more subtly integrated, lighter and more refined, and fireplaces were no exception. At this time the materials used were more likely to be painted wood, stone or scagliola than the marble of Palladianism; pictorial tablets, or even Wedgwood medallions, are a common decorative detail on this style of fireplace.

Georgian fireplaces typically have basket grates with decorated fronts and cast-iron backs. From about mid-century it was common to have pierced metal fenders (designed to stop coals rolling out onto the floor); hob grates, with ledges at either side, provided a means of narrowing the chimney opening and helping the fire draw.

A highly painted chimney-board or fireboard was a practical and attractive addition when the fireplace was not in use. The original purpose of this device was purely functional – to stop soot falling into the room – but today a solid board painted to match a decorative scheme, perhaps using a floral design or a *trompe-l'oeil* effect, would be in keeping with the style. In summer, the chimney-board can be removed and the grate filled with bundles of fresh flowers, greenery or a collection of pine cones.

Grand fireplaces were often elaborately painted and gilded

A typical Georgian fireplace with restrained decoration

● Sympathetic reproductions of Georgian fire-surrounds and grates are now manufactured on a large scale: marble fire-surrounds are the most luxurious, but wooden ones are just as suitable and are easier to install; simpler designs are quite often the most effective

Decorative plasterwork was applied to walls and ceilings alike during the Georgian period.

The hallway in this late Georgian house retains its original fanlight.

STAIRCASES

In a Georgian entrance hall the staircase was an important part of the overall design. In substantial country houses you might typically find a top-lit central stair around which the room plan would be symmetrically arranged.

Staircases of the Georgian period displayed increasing lightness and elegance as the century progressed. Stone stairs commonly had a balustrade composed of decorative ironwork in the form of delicate foliage or scrolling patterns; wooden ones often had unpainted mahogany handrails ending in a carved flourish of fluted, twisted or spiralled balusters.

DOORS AND WINDOWS

The Georgian period as a whole is characterized by a transition from heavy detail to a more refined elegance: mouldings, architraves and glazing bars became thinner and subtler in detail.

Outer doors contrasted with the otherwise plain façade of the typical town house. Filigreed fanlights, canopies, pediments and ornate brackets are frequent features of a Georgian front door-surround. Interior doors, by contrast, were of panelled wood and largely unadorned. In a re-creation of a Georgian interior hardwoods should be left plain and simple, while softwoods can be painted or grained in a dark 'wood' colour.

The glass available to the Georgians was of substantially better quality than that which their predecessors had to use, and so more light was admitted to the interior. Sash windows are a typical feature of Georgian houses. By 1760 the sliding sash was developed; this allowed both halves of the window to be slid freely up and down. The largest windows were usually on the first storey, where the main apartments were located; on storeys above this the windows were smaller and squarer. Venetian (tripartite) windows comprising a central arched window flanked by two smaller, straight-headed ones, were also a common feature in grander houses.

WALLS AND CEILINGS

In order to recreate the style of the early Georgian period it is important to recognize that traditionally walls were divided into three main sections: the entablature comprising frieze and cornice (crown molding), the main wall area (with or without columns) and the dado (wainscoting), sometimes panelled and defined by the chair-rail.

A typical room in one of the finer early-Georgian houses was panelled (wainscoted). Wooden mouldings were added to give definition. In line with the general trend, the mouldings were bulky and bold in the earlier part of the century but gradually became finer and more linear. To emulate the style you could use painted pine throughout. Mahogany, used in the grandest of Georgian houses, is a costly alternative.

Walls can be decorated with wreaths, swags, laurels, acanthus leaves or trophies – obtainable today either as plaster mouldings or in the form of wallpaper borders and cut-outs. Ideally the design should be classical, based on either Greek or Roman models. This can be expressed by employing thick garlands, fluting and ribbon decoration; alternatively, a Neoclassical effect can be created very successfully using niches, coffering and friezes.

Ceilings and walls that were not panelled were often decorated with stucco motifs built up on wood or metal armatures, or with painted papier mâché, which was particularly suited to Adam designs.

- Plaster mouldings are undoubtedly the best, but some of the simpler, less ornate polystyrene mouldings can look surprisingly effective and are widely available
- Be wary of suppliers' catalogues when they describe mouldings as 'Georgian' – this can be a misnomer!

Ceiling rose (medallion)

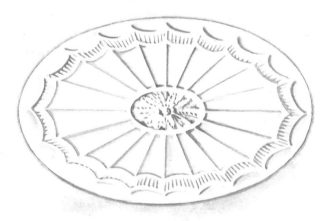

Scallop-edged patera

Cornice frieze with acanthus leaf decoration

Cornice frieze with anthemion decoration

Cornice frieze with Neoclassical decoration

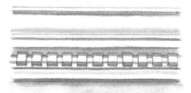

Cornice with dentil moulding

Cornice with egg-and-dart moulding

This room in Uppark, Sussex, demonstrates subdued, earthy colours.

The well-conceived effect of an eighteenth-century print room.

William Wordsworth's house in Cumbria displays walls painted in 'drab' colours.

FLOORS

The floors of a house intended to be in the early Georgian style could consist of bare boards; these may be either stained or simply left raw. In a Georgian home floorboards were cleaned with sand and rubbed with herbs. Today, you could protect bare boards with matt poly-urethane varnish. Some Georgian houses had plaster floors rather than boards. Coloured plaster floors were considered elegant. Grand rooms and hallways might have marble or stone floors, typically arranged in a keystone pattern. The large tiles are usually of a pale colour and the keystone is usually dark.

● Laying marble or stone floors is not always a practical proposition, particularly for apartments with wooden floorboards: vinyl floor tiles and linoleum (currently enjoying a revival) are now available in a variety of effects that simulate the appearance of marble and stone; suitable patterns might include a 'perspective' or a keystone design

● If you have wooden floorboards that are sound but uninteresting, you might consider liming them using special limed wax or undercoat paint thinned with white spirit; both finishes will need to be protected with either a wax or a matt polyurethane finish

● Parquet flooring laid in a geometric pattern would be appropriate

● A cheaper alternative would be to paint an oilcloth in contemporary patterns

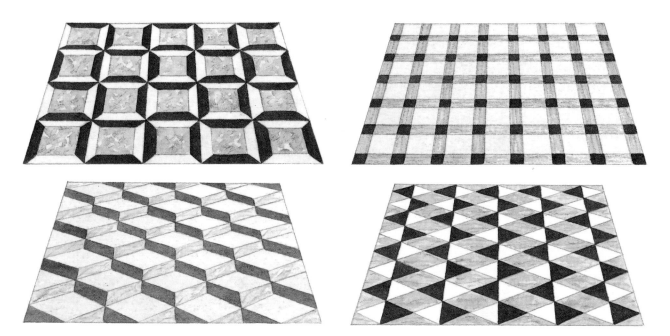

Geometric patterns suitable for floors

WALL COVERINGS AND FABRIC EFFECTS

PANELLING

As we have seen, the inside walls of early Georgian houses were often panelled. In grander houses panelling might be mahogany, but more usually it was softwood. Softwood panelling was usually painted, often to resemble a more exotic wood. Appropriate colours are the invariable dark 'wood' colour or one of the 'common' or 'drab' colours (originally a white lead base tinted with earth pigments) such as grey, off-white, olive or brown; following a later style the panelling might be painted pea-green, 'blossom' or sky blue. The popularity of panelling declined in the second half of the century, although it remained a common treatment for parlours and below chair rails.

WALLPAPER AND FABRIC

During the Georgian period papering was thought to be an appropriate – though expensive – treatment for ladies' apartments or intimate rooms, although wool, silk and tapestry stretched over batons and attached to the wall remained popular. 'Print rooms' were also all the rage – to recreate this style, walls can be pasted from floor to ceiling with old prints and engravings edged with decorative borders, ribbons, cards or bows. In the earlier part of the period fabric wall coverings were preferred in the richer houses. Fabrics to choose from might be dark silk, brocade or velvet. French textiles were highly prized and gave a special grandeur to Palladian interiors (see page 36).

In Europe (including Britain) the earliest wallpapers were imported. Originally, these were Chinese or 'India' sheets, displaying non-repeating designs of birds, plants or scenes from daily life. The sheets – each measuring about 3.66 m x 1.22 m (12ft x 4 ft) – came in sets of 25, and were very expensive. They were hung on wooden frames, pasted over linen and cartridge paper, so that they could be easily moved from place to place. It would be quite difficult to reproduce this 'look' today – though large-scale wallpaper designs, similar to the cheap English imitations of the time, with designs repeating in squares or stripes, would work well. Another type of wallpaper reflecting the Georgian period is flock paper; originally chopped wool was sprinkled onto a wet design to form a raised pattern imitating Italian cut velvet, but today you can purchase machine-made flock wallpaper to recreate this effect.

Other wallpapers of the later Georgian style (after 1770) were made of rag paper, block-printed in thick distemper colours to give a slightly raised surface; the printing blocks were made of pearwood. Shading effects were achieved with pins to darken the background. An authentic late-Georgian effect can be reproduced by trimming the walls with fillets or borders.

● Hang wallpapers that resemble the expensive fabric wall coverings of the period for a practical and cheap alternative

PAINT

Colour can be (and was) used to emphasize the division of the wall into sections. If the room is panelled, the cornice should be painted with the wall. If the room is painted, however, the cornice should be painted

Rough walls, painted a soft, chalky white, blend with silk curtains.

with the ceiling. Any woodwork should be painted with a semi-gloss or matt finish.

Other typical colours to choose from include soft grey, pale green, blue, pink and 'dead' white. Gilding, of course, is very important. Later in the century, rooms became more colourful, with subtle and sophisticated combinations defining the different architectural elements, sometimes set off with crisp white mouldings.

Georgian ceilings were generally finished off with a coating of whitening or crushed chalk; it is not too difficult to reproduce this effect with matt emulsion (latex) paint. The same cannot be said of the grand houses designed by Adam and his imitators, for whom the ceiling became the key to the entire decoration of the room. Elaborate painted or applied ceiling designs, in different colours, were sometimes reflected in the design of the flooring.

TYPES OF FABRIC

The great furnishing fabrics of the eighteenth century were sumptuous and generally expensive, but similar effects can be created today at a rather more moderate cost. In particular, the idea of *en suite* decoration, or co-ordination; that is, using the same fabric for hangings, window treatments and upholstery.

Silks, damasks, brocades and velvets are typically Georgian, reflecting the fact that at the time the French and London Spitalfields silks led the world. Fashionable decorative devices can include bouquets, ribbons, wreaths, garlands and birds. England was noted for its worsted fabrics, camlet (made from a mixture of wool and goat's hair) and embroidered textiles.

Oriental fabrics are another option, since these were enormously popular later in the period – in particular Chinese cotton calico and chintz patterned in bright stylized designs including fabulous animals and exotic plants. In fact, these imports became so fashionable that for a time they were banned from England in order to protect the domestic industry. This inspired some English printed imitations, often in blue and white – both because indigo dyers did not

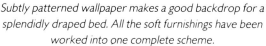

Subtly patterned wallpaper makes a good backdrop for a splendidly draped bed. All the soft furnishings have been worked into one complete scheme.

Georgian colour palette

have to pay tax and because the colour scheme went well with the sombre tones of the mahogany prevalent in grander houses.

Toile de Jouy was produced in France during the second half of the century. Usually this was plain Indian cotton or linen printed with engraved figures, flowers, birds and Oriental scenes in characteristic pink. *Toile de Jouy* is widely available today, in a variety of decorative patterns and traditional colourways.

SOFT FURNISHINGS

From the middle of the century, loose covers were commonly used to protect fine upholstery but were removed for social occasions. This aspect of the Georgian 'look' is easy enough to create, because the covers had a very 'modern' appearance. They were neatly tailored in checked or striped linen or chintz. The style of close

covering varies depending on the effect you wish to achieve. French upholstery had a domed, stuffed shape which suited the curved lines of the furniture, whereas English upholstery had more of a square profile produced by tufting. You might consider having cane-bottomed chairs fitted with tie-on squab cushions.

If you are lucky enough to obtain a really fine piece of fabric you could think of displaying it in the bedroom in the form of a bed-hanging. In the eighteenth century, as before, these were very popular not merely for purposes of ostentation but also because they provided extra warmth and privacy. Drapery can be suspended from a frame secured to the ceiling, or a tester joining the posts of a high-posted bedstead. The tester could be covered with an elaborate pelmet (cornice), stencilled, or painted with a wood-grain pattern.

WINDOW TREATMENTS

The tall windows of grand Georgian houses were often simply shuttered. If dressed, festoon hangings (forerunners of modern festoon blinds) were frequently used. A festoon hanging consists of a single piece of fabric which can be drawn up in soft billows to a pelmet-board (cornice-board), behind which hide the necessary cords and pulleys. To create a grand Neoclassical impression, the pelmet-board should be of carved and gilded wood.

Roller blinds – invented around the middle of the century – are another possibility. Originally the rollers were made of copper or brass and the blinds of linen, silk or wire gauze, sometimes painted or varnished. While you may not be able to match these materials, stiffened flimsy materials will certainly produce a very similar effect without too much trouble.

THE GLORIOUS EIGHTEENTH CENTURY
CREATING THE STYLE: GEORGIAN

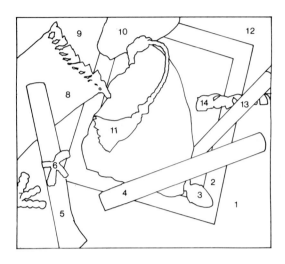

1 damask; 2 Georgian picture frame; 3 Georgian pineapple finial; 4 hand-printed wallpaper; 5 hand-printed wallpaper; 6 ribbon trimming; 7 braid; 8 antique damask cushion; 9 damask; 10 textured cotton weave; 11 cord tie-backs; 12 damask; 13 hand-printed wallpaper; 14 wallpaper border.

During the Georgian era, panelling, paint, paper and fabric were used to cover walls. Panelling was painted in 'drab' colours or to imitate expensive woods, whereas wall treatments favoured pale shades of green, blue, grey, pink and off-white. Wallpapers were much prized – from grand papers in the style of Renaissance velvets to simple, repeating motifs. Damasks and brocades were often attached to the wall with tacks and then finished with decorative fillets. Lavish use was made of textiles, with the best silks and brocades often being used for whole suites of furniture to create a sense of unity. Toile de Jouy was also popular, its pretty designs and soft colours providing light relief from fabrics in more sombre tones. Loose covers were made from practical, hard-wearing fabrics such as ticking or striped linen, with muslin being used on many surfaces, from windows to dressing tables.

FURNITURE AND FITTINGS

TYPES OF FURNITURE

The typical Georgian interior would look sparsely furnished to a modern eye. When not in use, furniture was generally pushed back against the walls in the formal, symmetrical style beloved by the Classical architects, rather than being arranged in groups around a common focus, such as the fireplace or dining-table. For most of the time, therefore, chair-backs were out of sight, and so they were generally either covered with only a cheap covering or not upholstered at all. Tea-tables and work-tables were deliberately lightweight, so that they could be easily carried from one place or room to another.

Nevertheless, the eighteenth century was the great age of furniture-making. It was dominated by the English craftsmen-designers Thomas Chippendale (most influential during the 1760s), George Hepplewhite (most influential during the 1780s) and Thomas Sheraton (most influential during the 1790s), and by the architects William Kent and Robert Adam. Mahogany was adopted as a preferred furniture-making material because of its strength, density and ability to take a high polish. Chairs, beds, tables and so on could be painted in delicate colours.

Early Georgian chairs are typified by their low backs and their cabriole legs, ending in ball-and-claw feet. Gradually, as the century progressed, the backs became more upright, with the top rail extending at the sides in the typical Chippendale shape. Cabriole legs gave way to square, tapered

Chairs, mirror and curtain pelmet reflect the influence of Thomas Chippendale.

or reeded shapes. From the 1760s carved decorations reflected Gothick motifs and exploited chinoiserie fretwork, as well as Classical themes.

Sofas, like chairs, were generally set back against the wall; they were often curvaceous in the Rococo style, following the contours of the panellings or mouldings. The French *fauteuil*, with its padded seat, back and arms, was also very fashionable.

Then there was the 'Grecian' couch popularized by Sheraton. Original pieces are expensive to buy today, but good reproductions are a feasible alternative.

Georgian-style tables take many forms. They range from the gate-leg design and the D-ended table with additional sections to the pedestal tables that evoke the latter part of the period. Very common were small, light portable circular tea-tables.

Chair-backs based on Hepplewhite designs, c 1785

Hoop back

Shield back

Shield with urn-shaped splat

High-back with pierced splat

LIGHTING

It is hard for us to realize just how poor the lighting was in the typical Georgian interior. The fire, as has been noted, was the main source of light, but during the summer its heat was undesirable. Candles provided the adjunct and alternative. Dipped candles made of beeswax were expensive, while tallow candles, made of rendered animal fat, smoked, blackened walls and ceilings, smelled unpleasant and gave out only a dim light. All types of candles dripped wax, made a room hot and stuffy and posed a real threat to safety.

Modern candles are less of a problem, and can create a soft atmospheric form of lighting, perhaps boosted by concealed electric lighting. Candles are best used with Georgian-type candlesticks, which may be styled rather like Georgian balusters and made of silver, cut glass, walnut or mahogany. You could use candle shades. One form of lighting which became increasingly popular in Georgian dining-rooms after 1750 was the use of elaborate candelabra. To capture this 'look', candelabra should flank the dining-room table or be positioned in front of a mirror. Ormolu or gilt brass, both of which materials reflect light and so maximize illumination, are the usual materials from which they were made. Georgian chandeliers – for special rather than everyday use – were likewise often made of reflective materials such as silver and brass; many were in the Rococo style featuring cherubs or classical motifs. Some of the chandeliers could be lowered by means of a suspension cord; it was fashionable to cover this cord with red or green silk, trimmed with a tassel.

DECORATIVE OBJECTS

When trying to decorate a room in the Georgian style it is important to recognize the influence of the Far East: screens, fans, fine porcelain and lacquerwork were among the *objets d'arts* popular during the period. The Grand Tour was another important factor; people of privilege accumulated the works of Italian masters.

During the Georgian period the quality of glass improved tremendously, and this meant that mirrors were much used, both to provide a sense of symmetry and to enhance the effect of natural and artificial lighting. Placing a mirror between a pair of windows or over a fireplace would be a typical Georgian touch. The frame should certainly not be plain; Georgian mirror frames usually display elaborate scalloping or shell motifs, palm fronds, classical scrolling or Rococo filigree. Adam-style carving would be likely to include representations of wreaths, baskets and vases.

● Hang prints or paintings in formal groupings to balance each other
● Gilt-framed mirrors are a typical feature in a Georgian-style room, so look out in junk shops for attractive frames

CARPETS

During the early part of the Georgian period carpets were generally handmade and imported, and consequently very expensive. To be in keeping with the period you should therefore use oilcloths or small embroidered rugs; matting and painted canvas would likewise be appropriate.

In the grander houses of this period, particularly in continental Europe, parquet – laid in a variety of geometric and classical patterns – was the standard flooring. An option is to display an Oriental carpet in the centre of the floor, its beauty fully visible if you follow the Georgian practice of arranging the furniture around the walls. To give your entrance hall a classical and typically Georgian look you could lay a stone or marble floor.

During the second half of the eighteenth century the British carpet industry became established at Wilton and Axminster. Pile carpet became gradually more affordable. These carpets, thanks to Adam's influence, were often patterned with classical designs; they were generally fitted with borders to follow the contours of the room.

A cheap alternative was non-piled carpet, available in several varieties including 'list' and 'Venetian' (often checked or striped). Narrow strips of carpet were sometimes mitred around the perimeter of the bed to give warmth underfoot.

*George III candlesticks,
late eighteenth century*

*George II-style chandelier with eight
'S' scroll arms*

COUNTRY COLONIAL
DINING-ROOM AT
HIDDEN GLEN,
PHILADELPHIA

CENTRAL WROUGHT-
IRON CHANDELIER
OVER THE TABLE

CANDLE REFLECTORS
AND PRIMITIVE
DRAWINGS ON THE
WALL

PLAIN WHITEWASHED
WALLS AND CEILING

MUSTARD YELLOW
FOR FITTED
CUPBOARD AND
WOODWORK

SCRUBBED AND
POLISHED
FLOORBOARDS

STRIPED WOVEN RAG
RUGS FOR THE FLOOR

TRESTLE-TABLE
COVERED WITH A RAG
RUG

A SET OF WELL-WORN
PAINTED SPINDLE-
BACK CHAIRS

56

COLONIAL

CREATING THE STYLE

The term 'Colonial', when applied to furniture and architecture produced in North America, is very comprehensive. It covers the period from the 1650s, when the early settlers of necessity made do with furnishings that were either primitive or imported or both, up to the time of independence in the late 1700s, when sophisticated and beautiful furniture and interiors were produced.

Of course, from the beginning there were many strong regional differences in styles – differences reflecting former tastes and standards of living. For example, richer French Huguenots and some of the more prosperous British settled in the Carolinas and the South, whereas the affluent Dutch and Quakers, and the poorer Germans, Swiss and Swedish, made New York and Pennsylvania their home. All brought with them their own styles. Furniture, art and accessories were therefore based on an eclectic mix of primitive and 'folk' models, often gaily painted and stencilled, with more elaborate pieces imported from the homeland. In the first half of the eighteenth century, styles based on British models included William and Mary and, slightly later, Queen Anne. In the second half of the eighteenth century, increasingly sophisticated American-made pieces inspired by Chippendale's designs were produced. Similarly, architectural detailing became more sophisticated, again drawing on English models for inspiration, but betraying a distinctly American flavour.

GLASS-FRONTED
CABINET FILLED WITH
SLIP-WARE POTTERY

*A grand eighteenth-century interior at
Stanley House, New Bern,
North Carolina.*

ARCHITECTURAL ELEMENTS AND FURNISHINGS

Grand fireplace in the Greek Revival style, c 1750

Fine country fireplaces in wood and brick, c 1735

FIREPLACES

The principal fuel in eighteenth-century North America was wood, and so fireplaces consisted of wide, rectangular openings designed to take logs. Wood, also the main building material, was generally used in place of stone, marble or brick for fire-surrounds and chimney-pieces. The inside of the fireplace was usually constructed of stone or brick. Many Colonial fireplaces were fairly simple in design, surmounted by a plain panel of carved wood and sometimes often lacking a mantelshelf. In grand houses they might have imported marble surrounds or Neoclassical decoration.

Stoves were also an important form of heating. It has been estimated that the log-burning Franklin cast-iron stove supplied four times as much heat as an early American fireplace and it remained popular until the nineteenth century.

• Andirons are a typical feature of the wide Colonial hearths: look out for those in rustic cast iron or with brass finials

DOORS AND WINDOWS

During the eighteenth century, door and window openings were typically tall. The height of doors was given an added emphasis by the placing of broad carved decorative panels across the top.

One way of emulating the early American style would be to install exterior (or interior) shutters. These were, from an early date, characteristic of American elevations; they can screen strong light and insulate against extremes of temperature.

DECORATIVE DETAILS

Simple, robust and classically inspired panelling was widespread. In grand houses there might be egg-and-dart and beaded mouldings, fluted pilasters and entablatures. Pedimental decorations and sculptural brackets were common, together with a

Chairs in the style of Thomas Chippendale at Mount Vernon, Virginia.

central plaster ceiling rose (medallion). Many of these elements were executed in wood. In less grand interiors, the panelling and decorative detailing were simpler, often with no ornament.

FLOORS

Simple, practical bare wooden flooring captures the mood of the early American style – although, at the time, the floors of rural houses were more usually of beaten earth. Pine, laid in broad planks and dry-scrubbed rather than waxed or polished, is the best option, although you may find dry-scrubbing too much of a chore. Painted and stencilled floors might be interesting alternatives, perhaps with simple motifs influenced by the German or Dutch folk tradition.

At the time, fine parquet flooring was a status symbol among the wealthy. Some ground floors of country Colonial houses were made of bricks. Parquet is expensive, but the other two options should be well within your reach.

• Wooden floorboards can be painted or stencilled with flowers, animals and other traditional folk-art motifs

CARPETS

Carpets were a luxury, even more so than in Europe, and were very rare outside the best households. Aubusson, Chinese,

Classical-style shelving, c 1750

High quality period furniture at Hope Plantation, North Carolina.

Sturdy Windsor chairs in a bedroom at Mount Vernon, Virginia.

Persian and Wilton carpets were imported; more usually they were needlepoint or ingrain. For the less grand houses home-produced oval braided rugs, with rings of bright colour, and hook rugs, with naive designs, were common; modern equivalents can be made or, at greater expense, bought. Painted floorcloths – a widespread alternative to carpeting – could be patterned in geometric or checked designs. They are not difficult to make, contrary to popular belief.

TYPES OF FURNITURE

During the seventeenth and early eighteenth centuries there evolved a whole tradition of provincial furniture-making. The provincial craft pieces included settles, various rockers (especially the 'Boston' type), ladderback and arrowback chairs, and the American Windsor chair which, unlike its English counterpart, had a back composed entirely of spindles. Much of this furniture was painted decoratively. Chests made by German settlers in Pennsylvania, for example, were often decorated with stylized tulips. Simple, painted furniture is currently enjoying a vogue, with the result that reproductions are now available.

By the second half of the eighteenth century, Chippendale and his contemporaries served as the role models for North American furniture-makers up to the Revolution. Mahogany was the preferred material; in New England cherry was an alternative, while oak, birch, maple and walnut were used in rural areas. The availability of pattern-books and the influx of skilled craftsmen from Europe meant that fine cabinet-making was quickly established

in the growing urban centres of Philadelphia, Boston and Charleston. Of course, pieces by the masters are beyond the reach of most of us, but less refined versions such as 'country' Chippendale are still available.

LIGHTING

North American candleholder designs included stands with small circular tops and tripod bases. There were also iron sconces and plain wrought-iron Dutch-style chandeliers with wooden centres. If you search your local antique stores you may be able to find something compatible.

DECORATIVE OBJECTS

Pewter is a particular feature of Colonial interiors. Other decorative objects which would be in keeping with the style are rough pottery, wooden bowls and other hand-crafted objects. For grander, Chippendale-style interiors eighteenth-century French porcelain and English silver would be suitable.

Needlepoint was used to cover fire-screens and chair-seats, while home-produced samplers and vivid patchwork quilts were other common features.

WALL COVERINGS AND FABRIC EFFECTS

PANELLING AND WOODWORK

Panelled rooms or walls were common in Colonial America, so one way of creating an early American look is to fit wide tongue-and-groove panelling.

WALLPAPER

Wallpaper was expensive during the early American period: it remained largely an imported item available only to rich households until the arrival of mass production in the nineteenth century. French scenic and panoramic papers with classical motifs were very popular, as were chinoiserie designs from both France and England. American themes were gradually introduced: idealized portraits of Indian settlements and native fauna and flora featured among early American designs.

PAINT

To create the effect of a simple Colonial home you could have whitewashed walls. In general, however, paint colours in North America during the eighteenth century were much more vibrant and vivid than is commonly supposed. But bright colour in the interior should be reserved for woodwork and panelling, which will make a striking contrast to the simple treatment of the walls and ceiling. Rich ochres, dull reds, a whole range of subtle greys, brown and sharp yellow would create the true flavour of the period. At the time, paint colours were created with different pigments of an imperfect consistency. So to replicate this finish use matt paint, perhaps applying a dragged or scumbled finish.

Painted stencil decorations used as the dominant form of decoration on walls and furniture would create another impression of the early American home.

FABRIC TREATMENTS

The types of fabric typical of this period range from imported silk damask, satin, brocade and taffeta to plain cotton, muslin and home-spun. Blue resist-dyed linen, Colonial check, ticking, floral sprigs and flamestitch patterns are likewise suitable for an early North American style. Even in grander homes these fabrics should be used to make simple curtains.

● Curtains hung from wooden poles by tabs or rings are a simple treatment

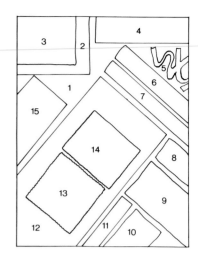

1 oak floorboards; 2 textured cotton; 3 cotton and linen weave; 4 cotton ticking; 5 ribbon trimming; 6 hand-printed wallpaper; 7 hand-printed wallpaper; 8 cotton check; 9 textured cotton; 10 woven 'needlepoint' fabric; 11 hand-printed wallpaper; 12 quilted cotton; 13 textured cotton woven 'needlepoint' fabric; 14 linen check; 15 textured cotton.

Simple festoon blind

Colonial colour palette

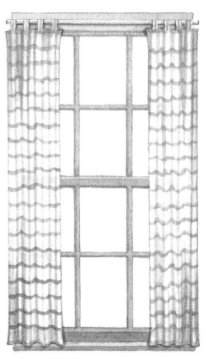

Tab-headed curtains

FROM CLASSICISM TO ROMANTICISM

French watercolour of a Classical-style sabre-legged chair.

Neoclassicism had come into general vogue by 1800. Its aim – to recreate or evoke the styles of art and architecture of ancient Greece and Rome – had of course been expressed in Italy and in other European countries since the Renaissance. For example, even when France was swept up by the extravaganzas of the Rococo, the nation nevertheless retained its hardcore allegiance to the classical ideals left over from the Baroque period and the nostalgic glories of Louis XIV's long reign. Likewise the British – and through them the Americans – were accustomed to the classical style because of the Palladian movement. A particular strand of Neoclassicism was the Greek Revival which drew inspiration from the monuments of ancient Greece.

Decorative plasterwork at the Russian palace of Pavlovsk.

Neoclassicism in the French Empire taste in a room at the Russian palace of Pavlovsk.

63

FRANCE AND THE IMPERIAL STYLES

Eugène Delacroix's 1833 watercolour of comte Charles de Mornay's tented Directoire *bedroom demonstrates the popularity of military trophies and draped bed-hangings.*

The French Revolution brought about great domestic changes. The building of middle-class housing, already increasing rapidly, now began to surge as industry and trade became increasingly prosperous and *La Bourgeoisie* triumphed over the aristocracy. Furniture, fabrics, papers, ornaments, floor coverings and wooden floors were produced in increasing abundance and very stylishly, albeit on a smaller scale to suit them to the smaller rooms. The new manifestation of the Neoclassical style was called *Empire*, in reference to the imperial phase of Napoleon's reign (1804–1815); it followed the *Directoire* period of Napoleon's consulate (1790–1804), which represented the interlude between the Neoclassicism of Louis XVI and the heavier archaeological style of *Empire*. Both *Directoire* and

Empire styles remained popular in both Europe and America right up to the 1840s.

One of the first examples of the *Directoire* style was in the luxurious Parisian house of a banker called Récamier, husband of the famous beauty Jeanne (*née* Bernard). The house had interior designs by Charles Percier (1764–1838) and his partner, Pierre François-Léonard Fontaine (1762–1853). It had wall-hangings of violet silk with a black border, capped by a deep pelmet (cornice) of cream silk with a gold border, and tall, graceful cream silk hangings draped behind the famous swan-decorated bed.

In the aftermath of the French Revolution and the Napoleonic wars, there were also many social changes, not least in the way distinguished designers like Percier and Fontaine thought it expedient to appeal to a larger audience. Interestingly, the devotion to Classicism was now more of a moral and intellectual allegiance – because of Rome's republicanism in the early years – than an aesthetic one. This was among the reasons why the post-revolutionary Americans, too, found it so attractive, turning towards the French version of Neoclassicism in a spirit of brotherhood and in gratitude for French help against the English. The spirit of brotherhood was, of course, greatly helped by the fact that the French drastically reduced the price of their exported goods to get the American trade!

In spite of the 'rise of the common man', as *Directoire* evolved to become *Empire*, interior style became grander and in many ways more formal. This can be seen to this day in the interiors remodelled by Percier and Fontaine at the Château de Malmaison on the outskirts of Paris, which was started during the Consulate and continued under the Empire. Clothes, however, became much simpler and a great deal narrower, as can be surmised from the curved Grecian-style day-beds of the period, which could never have coped with the voluminous skirts of the eighteenth century. Now, too, in the same way as just before the Revolution, the sumptuous apartments of famous courtesans became the models to which one aspired. Antoine Caillot, referring to a celebrated dancer of the day, wrote in 1788 that Mademoiselle Dervieux and the other nymphs of the theatre world set the tone of the boudoir for 'bourgeois

ABOVE An Empire *bed alcove with Egyptian sphinxes on the bed posts, an elaborately bordered Lyons silk wall covering and restrained draperies.*
RIGHT The salle de conseil *at Malmaison, Paris, complete with tented ceiling, spears, Egyptian griffins on the table legs and an elaborate carpet.*

women of the better sort and young ladies of quality'.

Mahogany, the most-used wood for furniture in late eighteenth-century England, now became the most-used wood of the moment in France (and also in America). Case pieces were massive, often with ormolu mounts, an insignia of *Empire*, and ebony inlays were a common feature. Swans' necks on chairs and bed-ends were very popular, and motifs in general use – apart from the military insignia, crossed swords, arrows and so on which had distinguished the *Directoire* – included bees, acanthus leaves, palms, caryatids and, particularly after Napoleon's successful Egyptian campaigns, sphinxes, winged griffins, torches and, used often for supports, Egyptian slaves and palm fronds.

Partly as a reaction to the heaviness of most of the furniture and partly because Napoleon was trying to revive the depressed silk industry in Lyons, curtains, draperies and upholstery in general became extremely lavish. In fact, throughout the eighteenth and early nineteenth centuries upholstered furniture was consistently more expensive than wooden furniture, and fabric coverings often cost much more than the frame. During the Empire lengths of tumbling fabric were festooned everywhere in a *dégagé* fashion. Walls were draped in all manner of ways, and tented ceilings were common. The usual formula for windows (and quite often beds) was a combination of heavy and light materials in two different colours, often with a third colour showing in the lining; silk and muslin formed a popular combination of fabrics.

65

A simple, late eighteenth-century sitting-room in the Lebell House, Kristinestad,
Finland, demonstrates the great appeal of Scandinavian style.

French wallpapers, too, were wonderfully inventive during this period; although they had started out as cheaper substitutes for the real thing – paint, fabric or wall-hangings – they were now often just as expensive. There were numerous versions of *trompe-l'oeil*, sometimes of 'fabric-draped' walls, complete with 'chair-rails', 'dados' ('wainscoting') and even 'prints' and 'paintings'. Painted *faux* finishes and plain coloured papers were used in conjunction with architectural and floral borders. In fact, almost all papers were used with single, double or even treble borders, or at least decorative fillets of wood or papier mâché. Paintings were produced for overmantels and to go above doors, and there were also elaborately shaded floral and romantic scenic and panoramic papers. Not for nothing were they called *papiers peints* (painted papers) – and not for nothing were French designs and French upholsterers (the interior decorators of the day, for they took care of all the furnishings and soft furnishings) so universally admired. The designs of Percier and

A cool coloured bedroom in the same house has a plain, boarded ceiling and floor, a charming painted border and a simply draped bed.

Fontaine were emulated all over mainland Europe – in Italy, Holland, Spain, Bavaria, Austria, Scandinavia, Poland and Russia. Between 1801 and 1812 they produced their seminal and sumptuous series of designs, *Recueil de Décorations intérieures comprenant tout de qui a rapport à l'ameublement*. Tsar Alexander I of Russia, a great admirer, ordered a set of watercolours of the work they had done during 1809–15 on the interiors of the Tuileries. Russia had imported a number of French and Italian architects during the latter part of the eighteenth century, including Robert Adam's mentor, Charles-Louis Clérisseau (1721–1820). The very pure, handsomely austere classical style distinctive to Russia is seen to best effect in St Petersburg (now Leningrad). Another Briton, Charles Cameron (1740–1812), also a pupil of Clérisseau, was chosen by Catherine the Great to work on her palace at Tsarskoe Selo. Cameron decorated the private rooms with a distinct Pompeiian influence, and designed a pavilion with patterns of agate and malachite.

THE REGENCY PERIOD IN BRITAIN

Britain, however, was starting a quiet revolution in design which heralded today's more relaxed and eclectic interior with its emphasis on comfort and ease. Despite its name, Regency style (named after the period between 1811, when the Prince of Wales became Regent for his demented father, George III, to 1820, when he was crowned as George IV) really relates to the period from the 1780s to 1830, ranging from the pure Neoclassicism of the Greek Revival to the fantasies of the Picturesque style and the exotica of the Prince's Brighton Pavilion.

On the whole, the Regency style was light and airy. In architecture, the Greek Revival held sway, as it did in Germany and America. Indoors, this taste for the Grecian manifested itself in plainer surfaces, a reduction or complete absence of relief ornamentation (with a resulting emphasis on painted decoration) and much simpler rooms. Many of the same Graeco-Roman and Egyptian motifs were used – the swans' necks, griffins, caryatids, winged sphinxes and so on that were very much the signature of the *Empire* style.

At the same time the Grecian couch was introduced. Since (unlike most furniture hitherto) it was designed to be not necessarily set against the wall, it started a more casual approach to furniture arrangement, as did sofa-tables (set in front of sofas, for writing or reading, rather than behind them, as is customary today) and round tables (used as a focus for conversational groups or for card-playing).

Being in fashion had always been highly desirable for the landed aristocracy; now it meant also keeping ahead of the middle classes, with their newer fortunes. When members of the aristocracy ordered a new piece of furniture to add to their collections – then as now, a room full of totally new furniture was the exception rather than the rule – it was usually a more costly version of a piece intended for the middle classes. This mirrored the situation of some 50 years before, when middle-class furniture consisted of simpler versions of designs prepared for the aristocracy. This profound change came about largely because of the increasingly broad appeal of publications like George Smith's *A Collection of Designs for Household Furniture and Decoration* and the influential *Household Furniture and Interior Decoration* (1805) by Thomas Hope (1769–1831).

ABOVE *A late Georgian sideboard, complete with brass rails and similarly styled knife box, is flanked by a pair of candle sconces*
LEFT *Splendid painted decoration in the Pompeiian Room, Ickworth, Suffolk.*
OPPOSITE *Sir John Soane's Pitshanger Manor, London, was built between 1800 and 1804 and illustrates his penchant for perspectival tricks.*

Hope was an interesting transitional figure between the old aristocratic patronage and the aspiring middle classes; in a way he was the epitome of the somewhat anomalous Regency, with its questing eclecticism contained by a Neoclassical framework. A prosperous banker with an overriding interest in classical and Egyptian archaeology, and a great admirer of the designs of Percier and Fontaine, Hope had a burning mission to improve the public taste at any cost. To this end he set about decorating and commissioning furnishings for his London and country houses, which he then let selected members of the public in to see – much as people

are given guided tours of stately homes today. Although many of his own furnishing schemes – which included Egyptian, Turkish, Indian and Graeco-Roman references – were rather austere, especially considering their eclectic bent, the detailed designs so beautifully outlined in his publications were widely admired on both sides of the Atlantic.

The other great influence in the early nineteenth century was Sir John Soane (1753–1837). In some ways he might be described as the last great English Neoclassicist, but in fact he was as innovative as Thomas Hope and somewhat more wittily eclectic.

Indeed, as his career matured, Soane added a strong overlay of Romanticism to his early Greek Revivalist penchants; his own home in Lincoln's Inn Fields in London shows extraordinary inventiveness, with its subtle top lighting and beautifully conceived vistas.

The Greek Revival in Britain was at its zenith between 1805 and 1810, and was particularly favoured in Scotland. Edinburgh became known as 'The Athens of the North' as much for its architectural leanings as for its intellectual ascendancy. It was, however, a style concerned largely with the exterior rather than with the interior of buildings.

The cult of the picturesque meant that major rooms frequently opened out onto a garden or conservatory.

THE PICTURESQUE

Romanticism, or the cult of the Picturesque, was also gaining favour in England. This started in the late eighteenth century, when nature and a romantic way of looking at it became very fashionable. Drawing-rooms came downstairs to the garden level, with French windows, or doors, opening out onto terraces and lawns. Buildings in what were now prized landscapes had to rest as naturally as possible in their settings, just as the views from their windows had to be contrived to best advantage. Haphazard asymmetry began to be preferred to the rectilinear lines of Classicism: buildings whose parts had been added somewhat randomly at different periods were felt to be very pleasing. Moreover, asymmetry had been the hallmark of Gothic, Tudor and Elizabethan buildings, the last two styles being quintessentially *English*. This was the time of the Napoleonic Wars, and so straightforward patriotism decreed that one should admire and emulate these styles.

During the Regency period the Gothic style found favour once again, based more on Horace Walpole's light-hearted Strawberry Hill home (converted 1753–76) than on James Wyatt's Fonthill Abbey. There was also a more vernacular interpretation of the style, adopted by architects such as John Nash (1752–1835), where 'Gothic' aspects were minimal – perhaps just manifested as pointed windows.

The Picturesque had, of course, immense appeal to those who longed for less formality. The English upper classes adapted the look for their country houses. Except on the most formal occasions, furniture was moved to the middle of the room and by the fireplace, rather than kept around the walls; often the loose protective covers were left on.

In fact, by the end of the eighteenth century the great English country house had become regarded as more or less obsolete. The smaller house or villa – whether in the Palladian tradition or in the more domestic and intimate Picturesque style favoured by the architects John Nash and Humphrey Repton (1752–1818) – was found to be more domesticated and intimate. At last people began to discover how to enjoy living in smaller rooms. The development of the villa, together with the changes in furniture arrangement, constituted a quite significant design revolution. In a parallel development, clothing likewise became greatly simplified, the cut being emphasized above all, and an English gentleman's clothes came to be universally admired and copied in both Europe and America.

AMERICAN FEDERAL

After the War of Independence the Federal style evolved in the United States. This style was inspired by British and French studies of antiquity and strongly influenced by the designs in George Hepplewhite's *The Cabinet-maker and Upholsterer's Guide* (1788). These refined the Neoclassical extravaganzas of Robert Adam. The American adaptations, however, produced a most individual melding of the two styles.

Cabinet-makers revived the habit of using veneer and inlay in predominantly mahogany furniture. Painted furniture was likewise extremely popular, whether decorated with the gilt, japanning, landscapes, flowers and trophies typical of the expensive pieces produced by sophisticated craftsmen or simply country furniture painted by rural artists. Painted furniture from Baltimore was especially prized. Carved motifs included the usual classical references of the times – the acanthus leaves, caryatids, winged griffins and so on – with the addition of patriotic American symbols.

An example of a Federal bedroom was charmingly described by Sarah Anna Emery in her *Reminiscences of a Nonagenarian* (1879):

> The best chamber was elegant with gay patch hangings to the high square post bedstead, and curtains of the same draped by the windows. The case of drawers was handsomely carved, the chairs matched those below and there was a novelty, the first wash-stand I ever saw, a pretty triangular one of mahogany.

The leading cabinet-makers of the day were three immigrants: Duncan Phyfe (1768–1854), from Scotland, Charles-Honoré Lannuier (1779–1819), from France – both working in New York – and Joseph B Barry, from England, who worked out of Philadelphia. Phyfe's work ranged from the Sheraton and Hepplewhite styles through to Empire and finally early Victorian, but his name is primarily linked with the Federal style.

By the early 1800s the graceful Hepplewhite and Sheraton styles were beginning to coarsen, in part because of the large influx of French cabinet-makers with their more pompous *Empire* leanings and their penchant for using Egyptian motifs like caryatids with stylized Egyptian headdresses.

ABOVE *Simplicity, grace and restraint were hallmarks of the Federal period.*
TOP *This octagonal Federal room has a central rent table, simple curtains, well-placed candle sconces topped with the familiar eagle and a handsome chandelier. The needlework carpet is well in keeping.*

71

The first-floor drawing-room of Pingree House, Salem, Massachusetts.

During the 1820s and 1830s, the new prosperity generated by the rapidly expanding economy produced a vastly enlarged middle class. Frances Trollope, somewhat grudgingly, wrote in her otherwise rather scathing *Domestic Manners of the Americans* (1821) that the 'dwelling houses of the upper classes [in New York] are extremely handsome and very richly furnished'. What the affluent desired most at this time was the sort of Greek Revival house which would exude a sense of stability and 'old blood'. The leading practitioner of the Greek Revival was Benjamin Latrobe (1764–1820), who had emigrated from Yorkshire, England, in 1795. Latrobe, primarily a Neoclassical architect, also produced the first Gothic Revival residence, near Philadelphia, for a merchant called William Crammond. Another influential architect of the time was Charles Bulfinch (1763–1844), a native New Englander who travelled extensively in Europe before returning to Boston in 1787. His extremely elegant buildings were

widely copied for the domestic market.

But perhaps no one had a greater influence on American nineteenth-century buildings than Asher Benjamin (1773–1845), a carpenter-builder who popularized the late Colonial style – a synthesis of both Latrobe's and Bulfinch's work – in his widely read book *The Country Builder's Assistant: Containing a Collection of New Designs of Carpentry and Architecture* (1797). He went on to produce an even more successful work, *The American Builder's Companion: or a New System of Architecture Particularly Adapted to the Present Style of Building in the United States of America* (1806), which went through six editions during the succeeding years.

All the same, by 1840, when the leader of the Hudson River School of Painting, Thomas Cole (1801–1848), was commissioned by the well-known architect, Ithiel Town (1784–1844) to paint a large canvas, *The Architect's Dream*, he showed a collage of Greek, Roman, Egyptian and Gothic buildings and details.

EUROPEAN MOVEMENTS

Mainly as a result of the enormous influence of Sir Walter Scott's Waverley Novels and his medieval romances, the Gothic style had once again reappeared all over the Continent – especially in France, which had its own particular version, the Troubadour style. This trend was greatly reinforced by the appearance of Victor Hugo's popular *Notre Dame de Paris* (1831), which in its turn led to the French Renaissance style of the Louis-Philippe period.

Italy, however, clung to the *Empire* style long after it had disappeared in its native country, just as Germany had remained attached to the Rococo much longer than had France. In 1809, Rome had become the second city of the *Empire* but, although there were many grandiose plans for transforming the city, few of them came to anything, and most of the best *Empire* interiors were created in Naples and Tuscany. The domed gallery of the Casa Borghese in Florence was decorated in a very ebullient *Empire* style in 1820, and equally exuberant interiors in the same mode appeared in Naples.

Germany and especially Austria were meanwhile being beautifully catered for by the Biedermeier style, a nicely simplified version of the richer and more ponderous *Empire*. Being much simpler the style was a great deal more practical and attractive, not to mention considerably more affordable – a matter of some importance, because the Napoleonic Wars and the Continental blockade had pretty well impoverished Scandinavia and most of central Europe, as well as depleting the supply of expensive materials. The Biedermeier style was aesthetically pleasing, with its clean, brightly coloured walls and small-scale furniture done in cherrywood, pearwood, maplewood, walnut and mahogany, often inlaid with ebony, or in black-stained wood.

Martin Drolling's Interior of a Dining Room *of 1821 shows a typical bourgeois interior where the emphasis is on comfort and practicality.*

EMPIRE-STYLE
BEDROOM AT
ARLINGTON COURT,
DEVON

DECORATIVE GILT
PELMET WITH SWAG
AND TAILS

WALLPAPER WITH
LAUREL WREATH
DESIGN

SWATHES OF FABRIC
TO CREATE A
CANOPY ABOVE THE
BED

TRIMMINGS IN A
CONTRASTING
COLOUR

TIE-BACKS TO HOLD
BACK THE CURTAINS

FRENCH WINDOWS
OR DOORS LEADING
TO A TERRACE

GILDED AND PAINTED
BEDROOM CHAIRS

EMPIRE

CREATING THE STYLE

During the time when Napoleon was ruler of France (1799–1815) there emerged in that country a style based to a large extent on 'military' symbols. Crossed swords, spears, arrows and torches figured strongly on heavy mahogany furniture, which also displayed imposing ormolu mounts, lion's-paw feet and ebony inlay. After Napoleon's campaign in Egypt, sphinxes, winged griffins, slave figures, Pharaonic heads and palm fronds were added to the design vocabulary. There was also a good deal of ingenious campaign furniture designed to make military camp-life more bearable, including folding desks, beds, chests and slim chests of drawers. Classical Greek and Roman inspiration provided languorous *chaise-longues*, curved swans' necks, acanthus leaves, laurel wreaths, caryatids and lions. The *Empire* style quickly spread throughout Europe and the United States, where regional versions of the style evolved.

Two centuries later it is tempting for many to tone down the *Empire* style as, seen in its entirety, it can be somewhat overpowering. However, the fabric treatments typical of the period – frivolous draperies and window treatments allied to drifting white muslin – can provide an important way of 'lightening' the heaviness of the furniture.

CANDLESTICKS WITH
GLASS SHADES

FRAMED ENGRAVINGS
OF CONTEMPORARY
FRENCH FASHION

Delicate giltwood side-table in a corner of the splendid Pavlovsk Palace, Russia.

ARCHITECTURAL ELEMENTS

Highly decorative finishes create a stunning scheme.

Beautiful paint effects in rich colours imitate classical mouldings.

FIREPLACES
In a room in the *Empire* style, the fireplace is not a dominant feature: as with Regency fireplaces (see page 86), the surrounds are very plain, almost minimal. However, since logs were the most common fuel in France at the time, elaborate fire-dogs (andirons) would be an authentic feature.

FLOORS
Parquet remained the most popular floor treatment for grand French houses. Patterns should be intricate but fundamentally geometric: lozenges, stars, latticework and diamonds are typical. Bare floorboards were more customary in lesser dwellings; the effect might be softened by simple rugs or mitred strips of flatweave carpeting.

Bronze sphinx with a particularly expressive female head.

DECORATIVE DETAIL
Decorative motifs were used essentially as a mean of dividing the walls into 'panels'. In terms of decorative detail the *Empire* style should be expressed by shallow, relatively plain reliefs and mouldings. Inspiration should be taken from classical Greece, Rome and Egypt; above all, motifs should be military in flavour. Originally, ready-made sets of ornaments, made of papier mâché or some similar material and decorated in *Empire*-style motifs, were available. Common designs and embellishments to replicate include laurel wreaths, trophies, imperial eagles, swans, Greek key patterns, lyres, arrows and bees (Napoleon's imperial emblem). The overall effect of the style should be bold and assertive.

A selection of motifs used for architectural mouldings and
furniture decoration during the Empire period

Lyre with ribbon decoration

Medallion containing one of
the nine Muses

Winged sphinx with scrolling tail

Swan motifs, the emblem of the Empress Josephine

Anthemion and lotus motif

77

WALL COVERINGS AND FABRIC EFFECTS

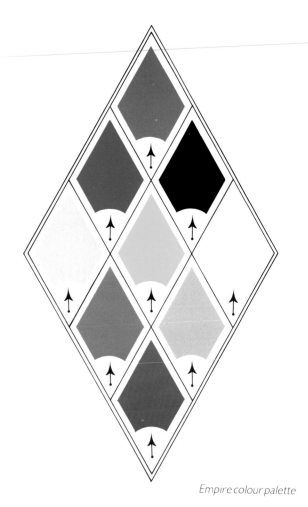

Empire colour palette

Wallpaper imitating silk wall hangings and a dramatically draped table dominate this French bedroom. The overall effect is beautifully opulent.

WALLPAPER AND FABRIC

Panoramic or pictorial mural scenes can be fixed around the perimeter of a room. Other *trompe-l'oeil* designs simulating marble, plasterwork, statues in niches and silk drapery would be in keeping.

Patterned papers should follow the designs of silks or chintzes of the period; this reflects the fashion of the time for coordinating the walls with the curtains and upholstery. Borders and paper friezes displaying classical themes can be used to outline plain walls.

In contrast to the severe lines of *Empire* furniture and the flat, minimal architectural detail, the use of fabric should be romantic and extravagant. Drape walls in fabric: it could be gathered in folds and bunches and held back to reveal mirrors or windows. Pleat the material: this will help to create the opulence typical of *Empire* fabric treatments.

White muslin drapery has a purity which makes it naturally associated with the rational spirit of Classicism that was so in vogue at the time. Muslin can be used informally in an asymmetric way, draping niches and festooning furniture. Satin in bright green, yellow and crimson is typically *Empire*; satins can be bought either plain or with small repeat designs, often in gold.

You could also consider creating a tented room, with the walls and ceiling totally enclosed in fabric. In the early *Empire* these were masculine in style, suggesting military campaign tents, but later they became more 'feminine', displaying exotic Turkish influences in the style of their trimmings and finish.

- Use stencilled *Empire* motifs such as lyres, stars, sphinxes, palmettes, caryatids

- Architectural detail is applied rather than intrinsic to an *Empire* scheme, so make use of the wide variety of stunning paper borders and friezes that are available today
- Paper that imitates swagged drapery looks effective, particularly when finished off with an elaborate 'fabric' border
- Even when used in small quantities, either to cover a footstool or a cushion, luxurious, brightly coloured silks successfully sum up the *Empire* style
- Tented rooms can be made to resemble campaign tents by using fabric with bold stripes; striped paper applied to the walls and across the ceiling will give a similar effect
- Butter muslin undercurtains are cheap and allow maximum light into a room; for additional privacy you can incorporate a roller blind in a coordinating colour to match the pelmet

PAINT

The fashion had persisted throughout the second half of the eighteenth century for painted 'grotesques', following the discovery of similar paintings in ancient ruins, or 'grottoes' during the Renaissance. This, in turn, gave rise to the Greek Revival style of painted ornament, whereby inset panels or ovals depicted classical themes. From 1790 onwards there was also much illusionist painting: murals of idealized landscapes, classical ruins, panoramas and figures in gardens. Ceilings, particularly in intimate rooms or boudoirs, could be painted to resemble the sky, complete with clouds.

Graining, marbling and other techniques used to simulate expensive materials, are another important part of the decorative repertoire. Colours for the *Empire*-style interior are generally deeper and brighter than earlier: Pompeiian red and turquoise, set off with white or black, is a good combination; blue with white is also a sympathetic scheme.

WINDOW TREATMENTS

Paris was the leading centre of fashionable drapery, rather in the way it would come to dominate couture in the twentieth century. During the *Empire* period the correlation between costume and furnishing was very striking: high-waisted classically draped gowns in filmy muslin were echoed in artful muslin window treatments.

At its simplest, the style can consist of a length of fine white fabric flung over an ornate brass curtain pole in an asymmetric arrangement. More complex designs can rely on combinations of lightweight undercurtains with fixed outer drapery made of heavier material in brilliant colours. Both inner curtains and outer hangings can be trimmed with deep fringing, tassels or loops of cord. Brass *embrasses* (solid tiebacks) are a desirable feature if you are seeking an early *Empire* look. Poles, rods, finials and brackets of the time displayed typical Empire motifs, such as spears, arrows, stars and laurel wreaths. After 1800 the French rod, which allowed curtains to be drawn from one side, was adopted.

Painted muslin draped over gilt curtain finials.

Drapery designs were produced also for arched windows and for a series of two or more windows along a wall. The latter arrangement inspired a fashion for 'continued drapery', whereby the entire wall was treated as a single composition, with fixed pelmets (cornices) running along the top of the windows and across the wall in between.

Alternatively, each window could be individually curtained – perhaps asymmetrically.

Pelmets should take the form of deep swags trimmed with long or short tails. Additional curtains are not essential: roller blinds or shutters can be used to screen the light; these were common not only in France but also in North America.

Undercurtains against yellow silk

Lined curtains adorned with wreaths

FROM CLASSICISM TO ROMANTICISM
CREATING THE STYLE: EMPIRE

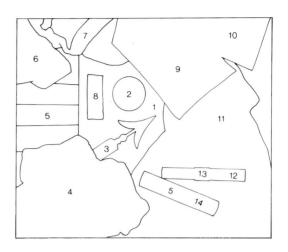

1 striped satin: 2 lion's head medallion: 3 arrowhead curtain pole:
4 silk damask: 5 wallpaper borders: 6 silk damask: 7 silk trimming;
8 silk trimming; 9 striped silk with laurel wreaths;
10 striped silk with laurel wreaths: 11 patterned silk:
12 faux finish wallpaper: 13 silk trimming: 14 striped wallpaper.

The severe lines of Empire furniture were counterbalanced
by the lavish use of fabrics. Sumptuous silks and satins in
brilliant green, acid yellow and deep crimson, trimmed in
intricately worked fringes and tassels, were swagged around
tables, draped over beds and flung over curtain poles. Heavy
pelmets became less fashionable as curtain poles and rings
became more elaborate. Finals, brackets and tie-backs
were embellished with popular motifs of the period such as bees,
lions heads and arrows.
Walls were painted or glazed in flat colours and decorated
with bold borders and stencils. Wallpapers frequently imitated
the rich patterns of Lyons silks.
The style is one of contrasts – black lacquer chairs upholstered
in the sheerest of satins, heavy onyx console tables attached to
delicately painted walls – but the overall effect is one of
monumental grandeur and luxury.

FURNITURE AND FITTINGS

Fashionable chair styles, c 1810

Throne-like armchair with
sphinx supports

Armchair with a
pronounced scrolling back

Armchair with carved swans
adorning the arm-rests

Armchair in a style derived
from the ancient Greek klismos

*Lamps, wall medallions, door treatments and side-tables demonstrate the
importance of symmetry in an Empire scheme.*

ABOVE and TOP Careful use of contrasting colours and materials in two French rooms.

TYPES OF FURNITURE

The development of *Empire* furniture displays the influence of Napoleonic ideals. This unified style was derived from classical – particularly Greek – architecture and, compared to the French fashions under Louis XIV, XV and XVI, was austere and severely rational in form. The pure lines of the *récamier* sofa epitomize the style.

Although pure in line, furniture should be decorative and may be painted and gilded; some pieces can have intricate mahogany veneering. Carved decoration is typical: the reverse lotus shape on chair-legs is a frequent example. Black was a popular colour among antiquarian enthusiasts and also reflects a renewed interest in the ebony boullework of the Louis XIV period, with its gilded mounts and brass inlay. Aside from classical and 'militaristic' designs, there are also 'Egyptian' motifs.

Beds are important pieces of furniture in the overall scheme. They should be elaborately draped and trimmed. At the time, although room layout remained formal, there was increased access to intimate or private rooms such as boudoirs and this increased the significance not only of the bed but also of day-beds and *chaise-longues*. (Sofas remained formal and architectural.) New designs for beds included the *lit-en-bateau*, which had a prow or sleigh end, and versions of an earlier style, *à la Polonaise*, in which a dome projected over a bed set against the wall.

LIGHTING

Oil lamps provided a relatively high level of illumination but were dirty and difficult to maintain. Various mechanisms appeared around the turn of the century, but candles remained standard. To recreate the style, choose gilt fittings that are in character.

Arrow-shaped candle sconces or a lantern-style hall light would provide suitable lighting for an Empire scheme

ROOM ARRANGEMENT

French rooms, unlike English ones, retained their formal layout well into the nineteenth century, with sofas and *fauteuils* placed in fixed positions around the perimeter; chairs could then be drawn to the centre to form circles for conversation.

DECORATIVE OBJECTS

An *Empire* mantelshelf is the place to display ornate decorative objects. These could include an elaborate clock (preferably under a glass dome) as well as black Grecian vases and/or Chinese porcelain figures. Mirrors should be used selectively –

although any niches and alcoves the room might have could well take a mirror.

Tiered stands and *jardinières*, holding natural-looking displays of fresh flowers – a development which first appeared at the end of the eighteenth century – look excellent in any room.

A REGENCY
DRAWING-ROOM IN
ISLINGTON, LONDON

SIMPLE CORNICE
MOULDINGS PAINTED
TO MATCH THE
WALLS

VENETIAN GLASS
CHANDELIER OF THE
EIGHTEENTH
CENTURY

WALLPAPER
PATTERNED WITH
GOLD TRELLIS

STRIPED UPHOLSTERY
AND ANTHEMION
DECORATION ON THE
SOFA-BED

SOFA-TABLE WITH
HINGED EXTENSIONS

LIGHT *FAUX*
WOODWORK

SCROLLED SOFA-BED
SET AGAINST THE
WALL

GENTLY FADED
WOVEN CARPET

PANELLED WOODEN
SHUTTERS FOR THE
WINDOW

REGENCY

CREATING THE STYLE

Strictly speaking, the Regency period lasted only from 1811 to 1820, the years when the future George IV was Regent because of his father's insanity. In fact, stylistically speaking, the period really extended from the late 1790s through to the end of the 1830s.

In Britain, as elsewhere, more and more small- and medium-sized country and town houses were being built. Ceilings were lower and rooms were smaller – but no less graceful – than before, and the furniture was scaled down to match. Consequently, there was a move away from the elaborate and costly applied ornament of the Adam era and a return to a more consistent use of Classicism based on increasing knowledge of the ancient Greek and Egyptian civilizations. The typical Regency chair, with its sabre legs, was very much based on the *klismos*, a type of seat featured on many Greek vases. The increasingly relaxed style of room layout also encouraged less formal types of furniture, such as the *chaise-longue*. 'Signature' details of the period include the Greek anthemion (a floral design based usually on honeysuckle, palmette leaf or lotus), the Greek key pattern, swans, sphinxes and winged griffins.

In the early 1950s there was a tremendous Regency revival. It was realized that the Regency scale was entirely suitable for modern rooms and that the style mixed well with modern furniture. The style has, deservedly, remained popular to this day. Conveniently, it is equally suitable for large or small rooms.

IONIC-SHAPED SIDE-CHAIR

DECORATIVE WALL DISPLAY OF PORCELAIN

Delicate architectural details on the door and staircase enhance this late Georgian rectory in Suffolk.

ARCHITECTURAL ELEMENTS

Ceiling rose with fluted edge

Rosette-style ceiling rose

Rosette-style ceiling rose with ribbon moulding

Ceiling roses (medallions), c 1815

FIREPLACES

Regency fireplaces generally had a certain austerity of line by comparison with their Georgian predecessors. Architectural detail is minimal, surrounds should be flatter and less significant, mouldings sharper and flues shallower. However, although designs are lighter and less massive they can be richly decorated with emblems such as gilt stars or bronze spears, particularly if applied to either white or coloured marble. Alternatively, Gothic motifs and detailing would be appropriate.

STAIRCASES

Stair designs were also simple, typically consisting of a mahogany handrail supported by straight balusters (which were sometimes made of iron). A circle of balusters took the place of the newel post. In addition to these spare designs, there were more flamboyant examples, where bamboo balusters created an Oriental look or other patterns generated a rustic Gothic. There were also oval, spiral and circular stairs.

WINDOWS

Around the turn of the century, the English adopted the French window or French door (known also at the time as the Italian window). This new feature reflected a change in interior organization. General living areas were now located mainly on the ground floor instead of on the first, and there was an attendant desire to link inside and outside spaces more closely. There was also the option of setting French windows (doors) on upper floors where they led onto balconies.

One of the features of Regency Gothic was the pointed, arched window, a fashion which stimulated the revival of stained glass. Alternatively, panes were sometimes painted to resemble coloured glass.

A fireplace with strong, architectural lines.

DECORATIVE DETAILS

The forthright mouldings and reliefs typical of the early eighteenth century would be difficult to reproduce. However, those typical of the Regency involve much more shallow features. The wall should be treated as a flat surface, barely broken up by narrow chair rails and friezes. Dados (wainscoting) would be in keeping with the style, as would be bookcases built in as part of the architectural fittings.

Ornaments to embellish walls and ceilings should be either painted or gilded. Ceilings typical of the years just before 1800 might have inset panels and feature designs painted on canvas or paper and stuck into place after mouldings and other *in situ* ornament had been decorated.

A variety of motifs and symbols can be regarded as distinctive of the period. From France's *Empire* style (see page 76) come griffins, swans, military emblems and imperial eagles; festoons, swags and baskets of fruit, including pineapples, are also perfect for a Regency scheme. Classical designs can draw on a wide range of antiquarian sources: Greek tombstone-top pediments and urns and Etruscan, Egyptian and Pompeiian motifs. Added to all of these devices is the still-popular Oriental style, especially chinoiserie, which took on a more emphatic form. Also, of course, there is the Gothic style to consider.

A scholarly atmosphere is created in this nineteenth-century study.

A solid marble fireplace sets off a collection of delicate porcelain.

Cornice frieze with floral moulding

Dado rail with cross-bound ribbon moulding

Dado rail with scrolling-leaf moulding

Cornice frieze with stiff-leaf and egg-and-dart moulding

Cornice frieze with Greek key pattern

A selection of popular Regency mouldings, c 1810

WALL COVERINGS AND FABRIC EFFECTS

WALLPAPER AND FABRIC

Both English and French wallpapers imitated the designs found in textiles. Look out for stylized patterns of fruit and flowers or more naturalistic themes. French manufacturers specialized also in panoramic scenes, often designed by leading artists. These papers, which were applied around the perimeter of the room, dissolving the conventional sense of space, were highly effective, expensive and much sought-after.

In addition, paper can be used to simulate those materials such as silk and marble which, during the Regency, had become increasingly expensive or difficult to obtain. Paper borders can stand in for architectural detail, giving a crisp outline and a neat finish to painted or papered walls. Design can include floral or classically inspired motifs.

During the Regency period fabric coverings for walls were, as before, expensive, and so they were more or less exclusively the preserve of the wealthy – and of the grandest public rooms of those who were just a little below on the ladder of wealth. It was recommended that fabric hangings should be avoided in dining-rooms, where they would retain the smell of food.

Fine worsted or calico were thought suitable for drawing-rooms; if using these materials you could opt for deep crimson, which was then a favoured shade. More sumptuous choices that would be totally appropriate for the period are plain satins, figured damask and, with its rich sheen, glazed taffeta. Tabouret, a half-silk, was used also on walls; this fabric had alternating ribbed and satin stripes.

- Paint walls in clear, light colours and then either leave them plain or painted, or stencil them in a simple repeat pattern such as rosettes; as an alternative, use one of the many wallpapers available in this style
- Plain painted walls can be enlivened by adding a decorative border or frieze in, for example, a Greek key design
- Canvas stretched on a frame and painted to fit in with the decorative scheme can act as a decorative chimney board when a fire is not in use

- Choose coordinating wallpapers and fabrics from the wide range of authentic printed chintzes still in production

PAINT

In Regency decoration the wall surface was often broken up by the use of paint effects rather than applied mouldings or ornament. Decorative painting achieved a height of skill equalled neither before nor since.

Suitable colour schemes range from unusual combinations of rich, lustrous shades to brighter, lively colours – these express the swagger and dash of the period. In the chinoiserie style, rooms can be decorated sky blue with sea green and pale yellow. In such a scheme the woodwork should be painted white or cream to offset the vivid walls. Picturesque or Gothic rooms, however, might feature untreated woodwork. Oak was preferred to mahogany.

The Greek and Roman revival of the early nineteenth century can be characterized by expanses of plain colour, enlivened by painted patterns. Pompeiian style, for example, can be expressed using flat expanses of deep reds, outlined by bold borders that are stencilled or painted on the wall freehand.

Braid covers the tacks used to attach fabric panels to the wall.

Strong colours create a bold statement.

WINDOW TREATMENTS

Divided curtains supplanted festoon hangings in about 1800; over the next two decades, rods, rings, brackets and finials became more elaborate and obvious. Curtains can be held back by solid brass hold-backs (*embrasses*) in the form of rosettes or leaves. The silhouette should be high-waisted, mirroring the fashionable dresses of the period.

Asymmetry was fashionable, and can be emulated easily today. For a dramatic window treatment you could feature flimsy muslin alternating with rich, darker fabric. The pelmet should consist of deep swags, trimmed with bows and rosettes at the tie-points and framed by long or short tails.

Trimmings, too, are very important. Deep contrasting fringes, loops of gold cord and heavy tassels make striking decorative details. Try co-ordinating curtain fabrics with the upholstery and even with the wallpaper; this creates an intimate, enclosing effect well suited to a bedroom.

- Elaborate curtain rods, brackets, finials and *embrasses* add definition to windows and make a bold decorative statement
- Use fabric bows, rosettes, swags, tails and festoons lavishly

ABOVE Opulent window treatments with a uniting curtain pole
RIGHT Simply draped curtains emphasize an interestingly shaped window

Although this scheme was created in the 1920s, the ogee-shaped pelmet above the window and the fine bed hangings emphasize the Oriental and Gothic influences of the Regency period.

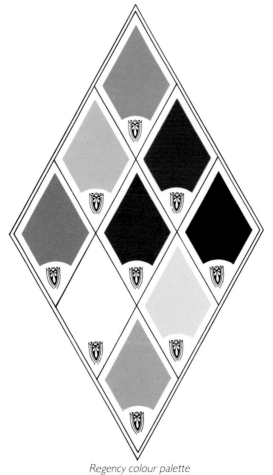

Regency colour palette

FROM CLASSICISM TO ROMANTICISM
CREATING THE STYLE: REGENCY

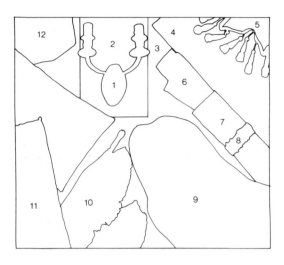

*1 Regency candle sconce; 2 textured cotton upholstery fabric;
3 glazed cotton; 4 cotton and linen blend; 5 antique trimming;
6 hand-printed wallpaper; 7 hand-printed wallpaper; 8 antique
trimming; 9 cotton weave; 10 antique embrasse;
11 antique damask cushions; 12 glazed cotton.*

*Regency schemes drew on a wide variety of sources, from
Ancient Greece to the Orient, in order to create the grand,
often austere rooms we associate with that period. Elaborate
wall painting in rich colours was fashionable, while
panoramic wallpapers depicting whole scenes achieved a
similarly rich effect in formal interiors. 'Chinese'
wallpapers created a suitable setting for the new bamboo
furniture. Damask and silk wall hangings, particularly in a
deep shade of crimson, were often used in formal rooms.
Curtain treatments were very important, with 'continued
drapery' and asymmetrical schemes being the most fashionable.
Swags, bows or rosettes adorned the tie points, while loops
of gold cord or heavy tassels provided the finishing touches.
Upholstery fabrics tended to be darker and more heavily
textured than in the Georgian period, though brighter loose
covers were used in summer.*

FURNITURE AND FITTINGS

A dramatic black-and-white rug accentuates the sturdy Regency furniture.

Yellow upholstery and walls set off an ebonized wood sofa.

Real and simulated bamboo furniture helps to recreate the feeling of the Regency.

ROOM ARRANGEMENT

The arrangement of furniture in Regency-style rooms should reflect the more relaxed, informal style of life that came to be typical of that period. The fireplace and windows should be focal points for informal groupings of tables and chairs, set up to allow different activities to take place in the same room at the same time. A pair of sofas can be placed at right angles to the fireplace, facing each other. You could have also a 'sofa table' (introduced around 1800), perhaps a rectangular or circular table which could be left permanently in front of the fire.

Light often determined where people sat, and furniture was designed to be easily moved from place to place; occasional tables and chairs would be set up near a window during the day, then moved near the fire during the evening. The new oil lamps gave better illumination and encouraged people to gather together around them.

The dining-room, by contrast, should be essentially formal in layout. To be in keeping, the table should be round and on a pedestal: during the Regency round tables, with their implicit lack of hierarchy, were more popular than rectangular designs.

By this time the library was emerging as an important room in better-off houses. Formerly a male preserve, it now gradually became the centre of family activities.

TYPES OF FURNITURE

Although original Regency furniture is prohibitively expensive, reproductions are readily available. Late Neoclassical pieces were generally lighter and smaller in scale than previously; the refinement and delicacy of Sheraton designs were typical. Table-tops were generally round or oval; chairs and occasional tables had narrow tapering legs; beds had delicate posts. The curving lines of the 'sofa bed' or *chaise-longue* were distinctive.

Mahogany was no longer the most popular material. Instead, in the best-quality furniture the warm tones of rosewood, often inlaid, were displayed, as were the paler shades of maple and satinwood; exotic species enjoyed a vogue.

A more robust Regency style can be seen in the designs of Thomas Hope, published for the first time in 1807. This 'purified Greek' version of Neoclassicism derived both its colours and its style of decoration from Greek vase patterns and architectural ornament.

The eclectic tastes of the Prince Regent were also influential. He collected French furniture of the *ancien régime*, particularly ebony boullework ornamented with gilt and brass. A good deal of fine French furniture was bought by the English in the aftermath of the Revolution, when the property of the aristocracy was being dispersed. Items from the Tudor, Elizabethan and Baroque periods

were likewise widely collected. The result was often an informal combination of styles. Mixed sets of chairs from different periods were common, particularly among the devotees of the Picturesque. There were also Gothic chairs featuring ogee-arched backs, with trefoils or quatrefoils, and woven rush or cane seats.

But Regency furniture could also be fanciful. Chinoiserie remained popular. Nelson's victory at the Battle of the Nile inspired 'Egyptian' designs, with the legs of chairs, sofas and tables taking the form of dolphins or crocodile feet. The Trafalgar chair, designed in recognition of Nelson's victory, incorporated carving that imitated twisted rope.

A great deal of Regency furniture was painted, often to simulate expensive materials. Table- and cabinet-tops were marbled; deal chests of drawers were grained to look like rosewood; work-tables and wash-stands were 'bambooed'. Great care was taken over the application of colour, glazed top-coats being placed over contrasting base-coats to achieve a deeper, richer effect. Black furniture, too, was very popular, often being decorated with fine line borders, fretwork or key patterns in gold. Chairs were painted with acanthus, palm wreaths or musical devices. Then there were colour combinations, among which red and black ('Pompeian') and brown and cream ('Etruscan') were typical. Particular attention was paid to the quality of the black, a rich shade being achieved by use of a green undercoat. Pale mid-green, grey and beige were used as background colours, with surface decoration in clear blue or leaf green.

DECORATIVE OBJECTS

Grecian urns, Chinese porcelain, antiquarian artefacts or Gothic curios are suitable accessories for the Regency style. Paintings hung in vertical rows on satin ribbons provide another hallmark of the Regency style. Small oval or round mirrors, with gilt frames crowned with wreaths, eagles or trophies, add a further authentic touch.

CARPETS

Carpet was much more widespread in England than in the previous period. Generally a margin of floor was left uncovered around the perimeter of the room.

For less wealthy households, and for the non-public rooms in grander ones, carpet substitutes were very important. Oilcloth was the chief alternative and was often painted with charming pictorial designs or in simulation of real materials or carpet patterns. Matting was also popular.

Created during the 1960s, this room combines Empire-influenced furniture with softer, Regency colours.

Popular forms of brass Regency lighting

Chandelier with six 'S' scroll arms

Lantern light, commonly used in hallways

Candle sconce with urn decoration

THE DRAWING-ROOM
OF PINGREE HOUSE,
SALEM,
MASSACHUSETTS,
DESIGNED BY SAMUEL
McINTIRE IN 1804

CORNICE MOULDING
PICKED OUT IN
COLOUR

PAINTED FRIEZE
ABOVE THE DADO
AND AROUND THE
WINDOW FRAMES

CURTAIN POLES WITH
FINIALS

ASYMMETRICAL
WINDOW
TREATMENTS IN
PRINTED MUSLIN

SMALL REPEAT MOTIF
ON MUSTARD
YELLOW WALLPAPER

POLISHED WOODEN
FLOORBOARDS WITH
A WOVEN CARPET

OPEN HEARTH WITH
ANDIRONS

BIRD'S-EYE MIRROR
WITH THE PATRIOTIC
EAGLE

FEDERAL

CREATING THE STYLE

The Federal style flourished in the United States in the late eighteenth and early nineteenth centuries. It has long been a favourite American style and, with the burgeoning of restoration and the new passion for old houses, Federal furnishings are highly prized. Above all, the style is elegant and refined. Drawing upon the designs of Sheraton and Hepplewhite, the early Regency in Britain, and the *Directoire* and early *Empire* in France, the style became known in its declining years as American Empire. Post-revolutionary American interior decoration, just like French *Empire*, included the classical motifs of ancient Greece and Rome, using these motifs alongside its own eagle as symbols of the new Federal government. As a token of brotherhood with the French Revolution, American cabinet-makers like Duncan Phyfe adapted French designs such as the lyre-backed chair and the caryatid-based console.

Federal furniture is generally made of mahogany, rosewood, cherry or bird's-eye maple. Mahogany furniture, in particular, may be decorated with veneer and inlay. There is also much painted furniture from this period. Soft-furnishing materials typical of the period include taffetas, silks, brocades and *toiles de Jouy*, reproductions of which are available today.

Late Federal staircase at Bacon House,
Washington, DC.

HEPPLEWHITE-STYLE
DINING-CHAIRS AND
CARD-TABLES

SILVER CANDLESTICKS
WITH WHITE CANDLES

ARCHITECTURAL ELEMENTS

FIREPLACES

During the early Federal period there was still a strong Adam influence on fireplace design. Later fireplaces became more reminiscent of France's *Empire* style. The eagle, adopted as the American symbol of the New Republic, was a common embellishment, along with other local motifs such as wheatsheaves and baskets of fruit. Fire surrounds were usually made of wood.

The famous pot-belly stoves were also a common sight in the Federal interior. The descendants of such stoves are available today and can be installed at quite a reasonable cost, but you will also need a good, reliable flue system.

LEFT Cobalt blue woodwork and plain white walls create a suitable setting for this charming Federal bed.
OPPOSITE LEFT Black-and-white tiles set off a fine collection of Federal furniture.
OPPOSITE ABOVE RIGHT and OPPOSITE BELOW RIGHT A sense of unity is cleverly created in this large hallway: the same cool blue colour is used throughout the lower floor. Beautiful silk rugs lead us from the hallway into the rest of the house and a gilt mirror follows the shape of the door frame.

Adam-style wooden fire surround, c 1795

Wooden fire surround, with eagle decoration, c 1800

DECORATIVE DETAILS

Whereas the Colonial style is somewhat heavy, Federal style is more delicate and linear. The overall effect is, however, much simpler than its English equivalent. Architraves and relief decorations are often very shallow, barely projecting from the surface of the wall. Small-scale linear patterns are common and simple geometric shapes such as ovals, circles and squares are often incorporated. At the time, this purity of line had the additional advantage that decoration could be executed very easily by local craftsmen, thus encouraging the development of a distinctly American 'look'.

Ceilings could be decorated with plain central designs in stucco. As in Europe, motifs were inspired by recent discoveries at Pompeii and Herculaneum; here the imitation of Greek Classicism expressed not an antiquarian interest but the patriotic spirit of the new democracy. An elaborate cornice (crown molding) might also be fitted. Motifs such as patera, festoons, husks, rosettes, urns and scrolling foliage, in particular, quickly became established emblems of the Republic, appearing over fireplaces and windows. As well as these, cornucopias were more widely used in America in this period than in England.

● If the room that you wish to decorate is devoid of architectural mouldings, you might consider adding a decorative paper frieze above the dado and around the window frames as an authentic Federal touch

FLOORS

Bare wooden floorboards are the most common flooring found in less grand Federal interiors, sometimes decorated with simple stencil designs. In grand houses, flooring may consist of parquet or stone laid in a chequerboard design – particularly in hallways – or sometimes in more elaborate designs incorporating classical motifs.

FROM CLASSICISM TO ROMANTICISM
CREATING THE STYLE: FEDERAL

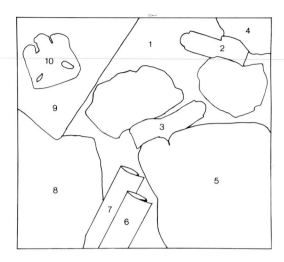

1 glazed cotton; 2&3 antique embrasses; 4 printed cotton; 5 glazed cotton; 6 patterned wallpaper; 7 patterned wallpaper; 8 patterned fabric; 9 cotton check; 10 gilt eagle.

Federal rooms reflected the new-found abundance of available fabric. Chintzes, dimity checks, silks and satins in strong colours such a rich yellow, crimson, green, scarlet and blue, were favoured. Chintz was preferred for drawing-rooms, wool for dining-rooms and libraries, with silk being reserved for the grandest interiors. Wool, horsehair and leather were used for upholstery, with chintz or silk in fabric matching the curtains being used to make cushions and other trimmings. Loose covers were popular and were usually made from dimity checks, ticking or chintz.
Wallpapers were used sparingly in combination with wood panelling. Papers with classical, geometric or floral motifs, often based on French Directoire papers, were among the most popular. The overall effect is of a more subdued form of English Regency or French Empire, providing a perfect foil for finely carved Federal furniture.

WALL COVERINGS AND FURNISHINGS

PANELLING AND WOODWORK

By the Federal period panelling was on the way out: in fashionable houses the walls were smooth and plastered – an effect which is easy enough to capture today. Also in keeping would be chair-rails and perhaps a low panelled dado (wainscoting).

WALLPAPER

French scenic wallpapers were still popular during this period, though now often manufactured in France specifically for the American market. Another style of wallpaper that was popular at the time replicated architectural details.

PAINT

The intense blue known popularly as 'Williamsburg blue' and the deep 'Federal green' are appropriate colours for this style. Grey, mustard yellow and deep lavender are also common colours for woodwork. Such muted colours had not been used previously and create a distinctively Federal look. For walls, white, cream and similarly pale shades would be in keeping.

A Federal bed, with its lace canopy and patchwork quilt, forms the centrepiece of this country bedroom. A double-chair-back settee helps to accentuate the rustic atmosphere.

Federal colour palette

A limited amount of fabric can create an authentic curtain treatment

Asymmetrical curtain treatments were popular in eighteenth-century America

FABRIC TREATMENTS

To recreate a Federal window treatment, drapery should be fairly elaborate. Formal swags and tails with draped pelmets (cornices), perhaps fringed or tasselled, would be appropriate. This arrangement might be used over simple muslin or fine cotton curtains.

Alternatively, curtains might be combined with flat or swagged pelmets. However, if you want to recreate a later early-nineteenth-century style, festoon or pull-up curtains should be used. Canopy beds were found in well-to-do homes and could also be considered.

FURNITURE AND ARRANGEMENT

New ideas about furniture and interior design spread quickly from England and Europe to America in this period. The patterns of Hepplewhite, Sheraton and Thomas Shearer (fl. 1788) provided inspiration for the American cabinet-makers, though designs were toned down, incorporating regional characteristics. Federal furniture is, therefore, lighter and more rectangular than its Colonial predecessors.

Mahogany was the principal wood; in regional areas indigenous woods such as cherry, walnut and maple were used. Technical improvements in veneering meant that pieces were not only more widely manufactured but also cheaper.

In the early Federal years, constant use was made of Neoclassical ornament. Other carved motifs and decorations including eagles, wheatsheafs, fruit baskets, lyres, rosettes, swags and feathers – in other

A Federal bedroom at Pingree House, Salem, Massachusetts.

words, a combination of patriotic and classical images. New types of furniture evolved during the Federal period. In the dining-room an important development was the introduction of the sideboard. Work-tables, with various divisions and compartments, also became a feature. Another well-known development was the sectional dining-table. In the bedroom, the dressing-table with an attached mirror gained popularity. Chairs reflected the delicacy and symmetry of the Neoclassical style: shield- and heart-shaped chair-backs became standard, as did rectangular and oval backs. Some pieces, particularly from the Baltimore school, incorporated small glass painted and gilt panels.

After 1800, Duncan Phyfe is credited with introducing a *new* lightness and elegance of design. Furnishings took on Grecian characteristics, and this came to dominate the last ten years of the Federal period.

- Club fenders are a useful addition to a living-room
- Brass *embrasses* with eagles' heads would be in keeping

LIGHTING

Candlelight remained the usual form of lighting during this period, but in keeping with the more formal style of Federal decoration, lighting became more sophisticated in design. Consequently, chandeliers and candelabra decorated with glass drops and multi-branched candelabra with cut and engraved glass shades would be suitable.

- Candlelight can be supplemented with discreet electric lighting, perhaps with floor uplights or recessed spotlights

DECORATIVE OBJECTS

Once again, eagle motifs provided a common embellishment for mirrors, chimney-pieces and pelmets. Mirrors, wall sconces, urns and vases all reflected the Neoclassical proportions and fine lines.

In the years after the Revolution, trade between America and the Orient thrived and large quantities of Chinese porcelain were bought to decorate the homes of the wealthy. The porcelain often repeated Neoclassical themes or could be decorated with portraits of American heroes.

CARPETS

During the Federal period, carpets were featured mainly in prosperous households. More frequently, carpets such as 'ingrain' and 'Scotch' were now produced in America. They were made in strips and laid to cover the whole room – often finished with narrow decorative borders. Floor-cloths, perhaps imitating Turkey or Savonnerie carpet designs, are also appropriate to the style, particularly for summer use in dining-rooms.

Chair-backs based on Sheraton designs, c 1800

RECREATION OF A
BIEDERMEIER INTERIOR
IN A MANHATTAN
APARTMENT

RICH, DARK PURPLE
WALLS TO CREATE AN
INTIMATE
ATMOSPHERE

BLACK-AND-WHITE
ENGRAVINGS IN CO-
ORDINATING FRAMES

A LIMITED RANGE OF
STRONG COLOURS

RECTILINEAR,
ARCHITECTURAL
FORMS

MARBLE ORNAMENTS
FOR THE SIDEBOARD

WATERED SILK FOR
DRAPES AND CHAIR
COVER

FURNITURE THAT
EMPHASIZES THE
GRAIN OF THE WOOD

BIEDERMEIER

CREATING THE STYLE

Between 1815 and 1850 this interior style was enormously popular, particularly in central Europe, Germany, Austria and Sweden. At the time, furniture which we now describe as 'Biedermeier' was commonplace. Its popularity was based more on its comparative cheapness, simplicity and practicality – it fitted in very well with older furniture (something which is just as applicable today) – than on any perceived elegance.

Better-quality Biedermeier furniture produced before 1840 displays an honest simplicity of form and detail. In origin, it is like Federal, in that its features are adapted from a mixture of Sheraton, Regency, *Directoire* and *Empire* (yet without the ubiquitous gilt-bronze mounts of the latter). Chairs and sofas are sometimes enriched with decorative supports in the guise of swans, griffins and dolphins, and carved detail are sometimes picked out in gilt. Case pieces are usually plain and block-like, and are often made from a golden wood like pear.

As a backdrop to this apparently light, simple style of furniture, the interiors of the period were equally bare and simple, a style which by the nature of its simplicity is eminently suitable to today's living.

A delicate Biedermeier chair together with a collection of portrait miniatures in the corner of a German room.

MATT BLACK
LAMPSHADES AND
SHINY BLACK BASES

ARCHITECTURAL ELEMENTS AND FURNISHINGS

FIREPLACES

In those areas of northern Europe where the Biedermeier style took hold, a chimney-piece might be built across the corner of a room; this contrasted with the contemporary English arrangement whereby the fireplace always occupied the centre of a main wall. In any event, the Biedermeier style preferred stoves to open fireplaces. These were especially common in ordinary homes and in private rooms; fireplaces tended to be found in the larger, public apartments.

DECORATIVE DETAILS

Biedermeier was the style of the bourgeoisie and was concerned more with comfort and family values than with the expression of grandeur, wealth or privilege. Consequently, decorative and architectural embellishments should be kept simple, almost to the point of non-existence. Walls should be plain, flat surfaces, uninterrupted by ornate mouldings or applied motifs. Any details should be classical, but in a much simpler order than those of the *Empire* style (see page 74).

FLOORS

In the grander households, polished parquet remained the favourite type of flooring. Contrasting woods might be used to create geometric patterns. Elsewhere, a standard flooring could consist of wooden boards, softened by carpets and rugs.

CARPETS

Flat-weave carpets could display cheerful floral designs; another treatment might be the use of plain, striped runners, laid in mitred strips around the perimeter of the room. At the time, machine-made widths would occasionally be sewn together to make a larger floor covering.

ROOM ARRANGEMENT

Biedermeier rooms display a preoccupation with comfort and domesticity which looks very modern to our eyes. In Vienna, one of the centres of the style, houses and apartments tended to be small, and so a way of

arranging rooms evolved which was very 'human' in scale. Furniture, too, was generally small and often portable. The prime concern among the new middle class was to create a congenial home where music, needlework and artistic pursuits, for example, could all be enjoyed.

The living-room was the centre of family life. To create the effect of a Biedermeier scheme it should be noted that the most important piece of furniture was the sofa, which was often L-shaped; typically it would be placed in a corner, with the other major furniture arranged around the perimeter of the room. In front of the sofa would be placed a round or rectangular table with a grouping of side-chairs, so as to form a conversation area. Further side-chairs (for visitors) and small tables would be pushed back against the walls when not in use.

Some pieces incorporated an early form of sprung upholstery, which was invented in

ABOVE and TOP A luxurious bathroom in the Biedermeier style.

● In general, furniture did not stand taller than the height of a man – a custom that increased the characteristic horizontal feel of Biedermeier interiors

Austria in 1822. Together with deep tufting and buttoning, the new invention promoted a sense of comfort and relaxation unknown in the drawing-rooms of the eighteenth century. However, more usually comfort was provided by ample padding, supplemented by bolster cushions.

Aside from the sofa grouping, the other important focal point was the window. Shallow platforms were often placed in window recesses, and on these stood work-tables for sewing, reading, writing or drawing. In well-to-do homes there would also be bookcases, and *étagères* full of porcelain.

TYPES OF FURNITURE

Biedermeier is largely known today as a furniture style rather than as a type of interior decoration. Furniture designs produced during this period reflected a growing middle-class demand for simple well made pieces and objects. Early designs are angular and box-like, but this gives way to the characteristic serpentine look, with curved chair-arms and scrolled sofa ends. Pieces tend to be symmetrical and geometric, with plain flat surfaces, often veneered. Much of the furniture is faced in light, honey-coloured fruitwoods such as cherry, walnut and pear, although birch and ash were popular in Scandinavia. Ebony inlay or ebonized elements make a striking contrast to the pale, polished wood. Applied ornament consists of simple classical elements such as columns, pilasters, pediments and cornices (crown moldings). Inlaid or painted decoration might be more fanciful – cherubs, swans, wreaths, fans, scallops and Greek key and lyre patterns are typical. But the impact of the designs rests on the beauty of the veneering which, after the invention of the veneer-cutting machine in 1820 becomes very refined on later pieces.

Sofas and side-chairs are the main types of seating; armchairs were not popular at the time. Secretaires – with fall-front writing-tops, drawers and cubbyholes – display all the cabinet-maker's skill.

DECORATIVE OBJECTS

A delight in nature is very important to this style. Windows should be filled with arrangements of plants on tiered stands. Groups of potted plants and cut flowers make charming and unpretentious displays.

To emphasize the linearity of the room arrangement, hang collections of small watercolours, prints and paintings in neat horizontal rows. In the original style, many of the pictures were produced by home amateurs and often they portrayed interior scenes or idealized landscapes. Mirrors should be tall and narrow and placed between windows; ideally they should have a classical appearance, with pedimented tops. To give that final Biedermeier touch, you could also display beadwork, porcelain figures and attractively engraved commemorative Bohemian glassware.

- A Biedermeier room should be amply decorated with flowers and greenery: line up potted plants along a windowsill, display a single plant on a flower stand or in a *jardinière*, or put a simple hanging basket at a window
- Hang pictures in horizontal tiers around a room above waist height, with the largest pictures in the top row and those in lower tiers progressively smaller
- China, shells, wooden boxes and other trinkets arranged attractively will help to create a suitably cluttered look

ABOVE A handsome Biedermeier desk.
LEFT Writing corners are a typical feature.

WALL COVERINGS AND FABRIC EFFECTS

A *Biedermeier* lit-en-bateau *and a columnar table in characteristic honey-toned wood provide a perfect setting for a group of carefully chosen objects.*

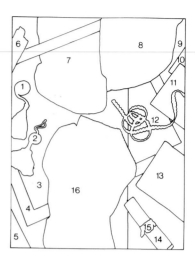

1&2 silk tassels; 3 cotton and viscose blend; 4 Biedermeier frame; 5 viscose weave, 6 horsehair fabric; 7 striped lampas; 8 striped viscose and cotton weave; 9 moire-effect weave; 10 moire; 11 lampas; 12 gimp; 13 viscose weave; 14 cotton and viscose blend; 15 trimming; 16 moire.

WALLPAPER

Biedermeier wallpaper designs have a charming, modest domesticity. Perfectly in style would be vertical stripes in fresh, strong shades of blue. As another option you could choose finer stripes and small flower repeats or a flecked design. A third alternative would be to have a painted wall set off by a floral paper border running along its top.

PAINT

Having evolved in Austria, Germany and Scandinavia, the Biedermeier style naturally shows an interest in light. Walls should be painted in clear light colours, such as pale green or yellow, and ceilings in white or grey – although in the wealthier households of the time they might have been painted in a more elaborate decorative fashion.

SOFT FURNISHINGS

Early Biedermeier furniture is normally upholstered in bright, strong colours, such as reds and blues. Plain woollen cloth, striped material and needlework are common fabrics. As the style progressed, however, drapery became very popular, and chairs,

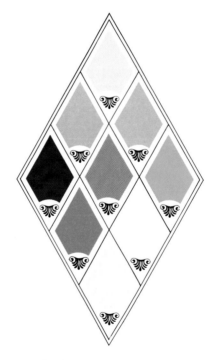

Biedermeier colour palette

- Paint the ceiling light grey or white
- Floral borders fitted at skirting level and below a cornice add definition

sofas and beds can be artistically swathed in lengths of fabric. Bed drapery has the practical purpose of concealing the function of the bed in rooms that are also used for daytime activities – as was done at the time.

WINDOW TREATMENTS

The window was an important focus of interest in the Biedermeier interior, and bay or recessed windows were very popular vantage points. Window treatments, therefore, although decorative, tend to be fairly simple, complementing a view beyond and admitting as much natural light as possible. The grandeur of Empire drapery and the intricacy of Parisian upholstery are radically simplified.

Biedermeier-style drapery should generally consist of plain (rather than patterned) fabric arranged in an asymmetric fashion over brass rods; tassels, fringes and draped pelmets (cornices) are appropriate embellishments. Alternatively, you could have a pair of white or pale muslin curtains, hung very simply from a brass rod and trimmed with a white netted fringe. For a more dramatic effect, add black fringing.

THE VICTORIAN AGE

Queen Victoria's reign in Britain began in 1837, and continued until the first year of the twentieth century. Britain, with its thriving industry and many colonies, was enormously prosperous. Similarly, France and the United States became extremely wealthy, again as a direct result of the entrepreneurial possibilities presented by the Industrial Revolution. In order to meet the demands of a rapidly expanding, socially aspiring population, architects and designers often plundered the past for inspiration. The main styles to regain popularity were neo-Rococo, Gothic, and neo-Renaissance. Other styles, such as Scottish Baronial and Moorish all had their moments of glory. The styles ebbed and flowed in popularity, often co-existing with one another.

Decorative tie-back of the nineteenth century.

Plasterwork in the hallway of a Victorian house.

The spectacularly over-stuffed drawing room of the Linley Sambourne House, London.

THE VICTORIAN HOUSE

In the first half of the nineteenth century the swelling size of households, the rapidly burgeoning middle classes and their demand for new houses to proclaim their social position and means put enormous pressure on the already overcrowded cities, driving people of adequate means out to the fringes, and further. This move also distanced them from the disease-ridden slums and the working classes, altogether desirable if they were to make their new status more noticeable. New towns and suburbs sprang up wherever seemed practicable, because of the location nearby of a centre of commerce and industry or the convenience of a station on the recently constructed railway lines. Since space and time were at a premium, particularly in Britain, building terraces of houses with tall, narrow fronts seemed the most appropriate solution.

In the United States, after the Civil War ended in 1865, people looked to the future with the same optimism as the Victorian British. Railways spread throughout the nation, uniting the more remote regions. The increasingly prosperous, upwardly mobile middle classes contributed to a substantial upper class, whose enormous wealth was based not on land, as in Europe, but on sheer economic ability. This new, rich élite of railroad, industrial and banking magnates pursued the building and furnishing of their luxurious mansions with dedicated zeal. For them, just as for the new middle classes everywhere, the more sumptuous and extravagant the mansion, the more awesome the outward sign of success.

DESIGN AND LAYOUT

The new generation of white-collar workers required that their homes portray an image of substance, respectability and taste as well as offer comfort and privacy. Although the basic design of terraced (row) houses was classical or (particularly in Britain) Georgian, they were embellished with ostentatious details from a variety of styles which sought to emulate those of the aristocracy. In the first half of the nineteenth century houses were designed frequently with elements of the neo-Renaissance or neo-Gothic styles.

Many mid-nineteenth-century terraced (row) houses generally had four floors, plus a basement and attic, with two large rooms on each floor. The basement contained the kitchen and servants' living quarters. The hallway, dining-room and parlour were on the ground floor, the drawing-room and morning-room on the first floor, and the bedrooms on the upper floors. Children slept together, girls in one room and boys in the other; servants and babies slept in the attic. Before 1870 few houses had bathrooms.

The hallway was where visitors were given their first impression of the family's social position and pretensions before being received into the drawing-room. There would be high ceilings (adorned with plasterwork and brackets), elaborate panelling, pictures and ornaments, and a staircase wider at the bottom than in the higher, invisible regions of the house.

The drawing-room itself, at the front of the house, was the main reception room and was heavily equipped with the family's best furniture. The morning-room, at

Enormous numbers of new houses were built in the Victorian age — new towns and suburbs appeared everywhere. Fancy iron and woodwork, as in this Texan house (above), were much favoured in America and Australia. This semi-detached house (left) was typical of thousands lining new streets throughout Britain.

Balloon-back chairs help to create the early Victorian atmosphere of
P.C. Wonder's Three Ladies in a Drawing Room *of c 1830.*

the back of the house, was the room where breakfast was taken as well as the focus of family activity. These rooms were often connected by folding or sliding doors. In France and the United States, where the emphasis was on entertainment, rooms opened out onto each other, but in Britain, where the preference was for privacy, rooms were frequently given separate access.

FURNISHINGS

The drawing- and morning-rooms were filled with plump, large, deeply buttoned and lavishly trimmed sofas, easy chairs, pouffes and ottomans; coil springing, developed in the 1850s, increased the comfort of these items of furniture. Japanned papier mâché chair-backs were frequently inlaid with mother-of-pearl or painted with landscapes. Thanks to the recent invention of the Jacquard loom (1801–1808), upholstery was highly patterned; improved machine-weaving had the same effect on carpets, which were often covered with three-dimensional designs. Heavy drapery festooned every possible surface – pelmets (cornices), mantelpieces, door lintels and tables. In summer much of the drapery tended to be cotton, muslin or chintz; in the colder months velvet or damask would be used instead. Wallpaper, now produced in rolls, was richly patterned

with flowers, birds or trellises. Those surfaces that were not covered were marbled, stained or stencilled. The level of decoration in the bedrooms was a little lighter and more restrained, with rag rugs or oilcloths thrown over deal or stained floorboards.

Plants and ornaments were everywhere: glass domes – covering homemade arrangements of silk, wool or wax flowers or stuffed animals and birds – adorned every mantelpiece, as did pairs of china dogs and porcelain figurines. Since women and girls had plenty of leisure time, embroidery, needlepoint and lacework were widespread on cushions, foot-stools and firescreens.

During the early Victorian period the popular colours were crimson and bottle green. When chemical dyes were developed in the 1850s, brighter colours were introduced, principally purple, Prussian blue, yellow and green. However, this new brilliance could do little to lighten the overall gloom prevalent during both day and night: the window treatments cut out a lot of sunlight, and artificial illumination was generally poor: paraffin (kerosene) lamps were introduced only in the 1860s, and gas lighting was not common until 1900. The overcrowded Victorian room was regarded as a gentle-manly and Christian reflection of a family's means and a necessary statement of respectability.

VICTORIAN STYLES

*In the nineteenth century, the grand appearance of this kind of French interior was
admired and emulated throughout Europe and the United States.*

RAMPANT ECLECTICISM

If the Victorian age was characterized by the large and
closely knit family, it was also the age of eclecticism. It
saw the revival of romantic styles and, more academic-
ally, of antiquarianism and historicism. An increase in
the number of people who travelled, the employment of
thousands of people in the colonial services, the military struggles in India, Sudan, Africa, South Africa, the
Crimea and China — all led to an interest in styles other
than the classical. Whereas in the eighteenth century a
somewhat flippant tongue-in-cheek attitude to non-
classical styles had prevailed, now every style was taken
most seriously.

In the homes of the rich – from Detroit to New
York, Prague to Paris, Stockholm to London – Empire
Classicism fought with neo-Rococo (or Second Rococo,
as it was called in the United States), Baroque, French
and Italian Renaissance, Moorish, Egyptian, Oriental
and Gothic. These styles were either recreated as
authentically as possible by determined historicists or
carefully compiled by the cultivated rich from actual
elements of old European rooms; some wealthy Americans even managed to transplant whole rooms across the
Atlantic. More often, though, styles were merely
approximated, using loose interpretations of largely
European models.

People turned frequently to new styles in order to
stay ahead: the more lavish and difficult to copy the
better. It was not unusual for the wealthy and powerful
to have different houses decorated in different styles or
even to combine styles in the same house. Rococo was
considered suitable for bedrooms, boudoirs and drawing-rooms, whereas Gothic was appropriate for libraries,
dining-rooms and other male preserves. Queen Victoria
herself chose Scottish Baronial for Balmoral and Tuscan
Renaissance for Osborne, her home in the Isle of
Wight. The extraordinary fantasy palaces of Ludwig II
of Bavaria were likewise each decorated differently –
Neuschwanstein is a Gothic/Byzantine confection,
Linderhof is Baroque and Herrenchiemsee is bizarre
Rococo, where palm fronds are combined with festoons
and the unlikely colours of intense blue and pink.

112

Rococo furnishings such as those found in this Brussels apartment enjoyed great popularity on both sides of the Atlantic.

NEO-ROCOCO

From the 1830s neo-Rococo and the French eighteenth-century styles were, until almost the end of the century, the most widely accepted for interior decoration. Encompassing the styles Louis XIV, XV and XVI (it was known also as the Louis Revival), the neo-Rococo was extremely popular in France, where it had political associations: Louis Bonaparte had become Emperor in 1851. But its association with aristocracy in general appealed to the socially mobile in the rest of Europe, Britain and the United States.

The style was light and cheerful. It was considered 'feminine' and frivolous, and so was reserved predominantly for boudoirs and rooms suitable for entertaining, such as drawing-rooms. It was characterized by curling shellwork and arabesques, gilt carving or moulded papier mâché, and mirrors. On the walls, areas of flock paper or silk damask were surrounded by pilasters or panels. The furniture tended to be rounded, heavily stuffed and elaborately trimmed. The easy chairs were nicknamed *crapauds* ('toads') by the French.

NEO-RENAISSANCE

Just as neo-Rococo was associated with taste and refinement, anything neo-Renaissance or Italianate suggested scholarliness. The designs incorporated rounded Romanesque arches above windows and doors, scrolled brackets and supports, balustrades, pilasters and pediments. The whole gave an impression of monumentality, which was entirely in keeping with the weightiness these classes sought to convey. Frequently the frontage of Italianate terraces was broken, which emphasized the individuality of each house. This style was made even grander in France and it became known as the 'Beaux-Arts' Style (after the École des Beaux Arts in Paris) and was adopted wholeheartedly; it came to be used all over Europe and in England. In the United States its opulence was particularly appropriate: the country's enormously wealthy entrepreneurs had become, to all intents and purposes, the Medicis of the New World. The style was also characterized by a stress on drapery. Banded fabrics and an emphasis on the horizontal were thought particularly appropriate.

THE GOTHIC AGAIN

The Gothic, which was more suited for architecture than interior decoration, nonetheless found a style in interiors. Its popularity in England was largely due to the extraordinarily prolific architect Augustus Welby Pugin (1812–1852), who had designed all the interiors as well as the exterior detailing of Sir Charles Barry's new Houses of Parliament and the Big Ben clock tower. While so much of the middle-class penchant for conspicuous display resulted in a deliberately eclectic plundering – a reinterpretation of any style that took their fancy – Pugin was a passionate historicist. He tried, with sensitive observation and meticulous attention to the scale and measurements of the original, to recreate the true 'feel' of medieval ecclesiastical architecture and furnishings. But, a perfectionist, he wrote sadly: 'I have passed my life in thinking of fine things, designing fine things and realizing very poor ones.'

The flat ceilings of homes designed in the Gothic style had ribs and moulded beams applied to them in an attempt to create a late Gothic vaulted effect. Furniture and screens were designed with pointed arches, and were usually made from oak or from wood stained with an oak finish. Oak, oak-stained panels or highly decorative wallpapers in brightly coloured Gothic tracery designs covered the walls.

In France the Gothic Revival was exemplified in the restoration for Louis Bonaparte (Napoleon III) by the architect Eugène Viollet-le-Duc (1814–1879) of a fourteenth-century château called Pierrefonds, originally built for Louis d'Orléans. Its painted curtains and carved panels depicting medieval themes seemed to anticipate the vegetal undulations of Art Nouveau.

In the United States the Gothic Revival was first made popular by the horticulturist, landscape gardener and architect Andrew Jackson Downing (1815–1852) with his book *Cottage Residences* (1842), and the style proliferated there over the next 30 years or so. The other manifestation of the Gothic in the United States, the Rustic, resulted in furniture of a peculiarly organic rough-hewn style, constructed from tree branches and roots. This had its apotheosis in Adirondack furniture, particularly used for the hunting lodges and mountain resorts in upper New York State.

ABOVE: An 1869 design by the skilled and colourful Gothicist, William Burges. TOP: The William Burges room in the Cecil Higgins Museum, Bedfordshire. LEFT and ABOVE LEFT: Examples of restored/ recreated French Gothic.

William Henry Hunt's painting, Woman in Jacobean Dress, *shows a room in
West Hill House, Sussex, decorated in a manner popular in the nineteenth century.*

SCOTTISH BARONIAL,
ELIZABETHAN AND TROUBADOUR

Associated with patriotism and nationalism were Scottish Baronial (in Scotland), Elizabethan (in England and the United States) and Troubadour, or *le style Henri III* (in France). The three were enormously influenced by contemporary publications such as Sir Walter Scott's Waverley Novels, which evoked images of chivalry and romantic love – as well as the more pragmatic suggestion, taken up by the styles they inspired, of a long line of well-heeled ancestors.

These styles were extremely popular during the 1850s and 1860s. Large, hooded chimney-pieces dominated the rooms, which were furnished with tall-backed, wide leather-seated chairs. Rope and bobbin turnings elaborated legs and rails, and twisted columns embellished numerous pieces of furniture from expensive rosewood to mass-produced pine bedroom suites, which were further decorated with brightly painted floral patterns. Walls were covered in wainscoting, paper or with wallpaper painted with medieval panoramas and hung above the dado-rail. Antiquarian interests were indulged in collections of armour, and the fascination of the medieval hunt was represented by the antlered heads of stags adorning the walls – particularly in that 'male' preserve, the library.

EUROPEAN AND SCANDINAVIAN REGIONAL STYLES

Carl Larsson's painting of his country cottage in 1885 shows a comfortable, pretty home furnished with antiques. The runner, mitred into a square, is intended to save wear on the floor.

In addition to the mainstream styles in vogue in Europe, certain styles remained concentrated in and associated with particular areas, such as Biedermeier in Germany and Austria and the Second Empire in France.

Biedermeier (see page 73) evolved from the French (First) Empire and took from it clean, simple lines, suppressing ornamentation, although greater stress was laid on comfort. The colours and patterns used on the walls were brighter and lighter than in other styles prevalent at the time, and the overall look was less cluttered, tending to austerity.

In France, the Second Empire was linked to a revival of Neoclassical *ancien régime* décor, and the results certainly matched American and English High Victorian excesses. Decoration dominated the architecture of rooms, as did *papiers peints* done in saturated colours and sensuous forms. In Scandinavia, revival styles dominated the second half of the nineteenth century. Parcelgilt and painted furniture, together with *bois-clair*, were used for all types of case-work, and especially for chairs. The painter, Carl Larsson, influenced Scandinavian design, with his light, comfortable interiors.

116

Like Larsson's paintings, this splendid dining-room demonstrates the importance of light to Scandinavian interiors.

AMERICAN REGIONAL STYLES

ABOVE *High Victorian parlour in Little Rock, Arkansas.*
LEFT *The eclectic Victorian hallway of Camden, Virginia.*

While the affluent on the East Coast were busy commissioning the latest eclectic styles, the typical interior of the rest of the hinterland and the Western states was extremely simple. Rural craftsmen made most of the necessary furniture, painting unpretentious chests, chairs and cupboards either in the cheerful Pennsylvanian Dutch or German eighteenth-century tradition with stencilled floral motifs of leaves, vines and baskets of fruit or in a 'wood-grained' effect. The most popular pieces of furniture were country Windsors, rocking chairs like the Boston Rocker with its broad scrolled plank seat, and Hitchcock chairs. The last combined Windsor with a rectangular back, a wide crest-rail, one or more horizontal slats and a square seat.

Another profound and charming influence of the time came from the various religious and Utopian socialist communities that proliferated in the nineteenth century, in particular the Shakers. Its members were required to relinquish all worldly goods and take part in a communal life that insisted on equality of the sexes and common ownership of possessions. The simply lined architecture, furniture, tools and utensils were meant to reflect a basic belief that creativity and work were forms of worship of God, and strict rules governed both decoration and the manufacture of furniture. Tables, chests and furniture in general were uncompromisingly and beautifully spare.

In 1876 the Centennial International Exhibition was mounted to celebrate the achievements in the first 100 years of American independence. This coincided with a new spirit of nationalism, which in turn provoked the Colonial Revival. Few exhibits at the Centennial were as well attended as the 'New England Kitchen', with its beamed ceiling, leaded casement windows and huge fireplace, furnished with simple country objects dating from the seventeenth, eighteenth and early nineteenth centuries. The Centennial led to a far greater awareness of the Colonial legacy in architecture, furniture and art. Manufacturers, ever quick to spot a trend, rapidly stopped producing their huge numbers of French-inspired Victorian pieces and turned instead to the reproduction of simple early American furniture.

A stunning collection of Shaker furniture made from maple and pine complements
the simple, white interior.

119

WILLIAM MORRIS AND THE EARLY CRAFT MOVEMENT

Wightwick Manor in the West Midlands provides a good example of William Morris's work. Begun in 1887, the rooms retain their original Morris wallpapers and William de Morgan tiles.

As mass-production and 'commercialization' appeared to spiral ever upwards, a movement emerged, intent on re-introducing craftsman-made furnishings. One of its chief exponents was the social revolutionary, visionary poet, preservationist, decorator and, not least, textile designer William Morris (1834–1896).

In 1856 Morris joined the architectural firm of G E Street. Here he met Philip Webb (1831–1915), who was to have a very considerable influence on him. There was no contemporary furniture available that the two of them liked. 'Shoddy is King,' Morris complained; 'From the statesman to the shoemaker, everything is shoddy.' So they decided to become decorators

themselves. In fact, the only furniture that Morris himself actually designed and made dated from the couple of years before his marriage in 1858. It was really in his role as an emotional idealist that he had such influence over the leaders of the Arts and Crafts movement (see page 146).

In 1861 Morris founded his own company, called Morris, Marshall, Faulkner and Company. It was financed with a loan of £100 from Morris's mother and was virtually a Pre-Raphaelite cooperative – with £1 share contributions coming from Edward Burne-Jones, Philip Webb, Dante Gabriel Rossetti and Ford Madox Brown as well as from the three named partners. The firm changed its name to Morris and Company some 14 years later, in 1875.

The company produced furniture, stained glass, textiles, wallpaper, pottery and metalwork. One of its most famous products, the 'Sussex' chair, is supposed to have been designed by Dante Gabriel Rossetti. Its ebonized, rush-seated form with a lyre back draws upon an eighteenth-century model. Morris's best contributions were his designs for flat patterns and his clean-coloured textile and wallpaper designs, which introduced a new and lighter inspiration that dominated the last part of the nineteenth century (see pages 142-153).

Although Morris preached passionately for the return of the medieval craft ethic, his objection was not so much to machine production as to shoddy workmanship. In fact, his first registered design was a trellis of African marigolds for machine-made linoleum (or 'corticine floorcloth', as it was then known); his first carpets, too, were designed to be machine-woven with separate borders of varying widths.

The most ironic aspect of Morris's aims was that, although he avowed to bring art to the masses ('I do not want art for the few, any more than education for the few, or freedom for the few . . .'), almost all the works of art that he produced cost so much in materials and labour that they were unavailable to all but the rich. His design ideas were copied by manufacturers who understood that the middle classes wanted to emulate the rich, and mass-produced emulations of Morris's style appeared in middle-class homes.

ABOVE *Morris's Red House, Bexleyheath,*
designed by Webb.
TOP *High Victorian Moorish style.*
LEFT *Cragside, Northumberland, completed*
1872 by Richard Norman Shaw.

IN SEARCH OF AN
AESTHETIC ALTERNATIVE

In the 1870s the Aesthetic movement (see page 144) gained a foothold as an alternative to the claustrophobic fussiness of High Victoriana. The two main styles that embodied the Aesthetic principles were Queen Anne and Japanese.

Queen Anne, or the 'style of sweetness and light', as Mark Girouard so aptly named it in his book on the subject, gripped the English and American public's imagination from the 1880s, although it had no definite style, reflecting instead an attitude in which comfort and informality were all-important. Archi-

tecturally it was defined by red brick, gables, bow windows, long narrow windows and lead glazing; it was especially popular in the United States because of its similarity to the early Colonial style. It was characterized by irregularity and asymmetry, calmer colours and a preference for antiques rather than modern reproductions. In England, the garden suburb of Bedford Park became the embodiment of Queen Anne. Devised by Jonathon Carr in conjunction with E W Godwin and later Richard Norman Shaw, it was light, practical and informal, with its roots in the domestic architecture of the early eighteenth century, but with its detailing and style of furnishing notably derived from Japan.

THE DRAWING-ROOM
AT PENRHYN CASTLE,
GWYNEDD, C 1840

LARGE WOODEN
CURTAIN POLE WITH
CURTAIN RINGS

CENTRAL MANTEL
CLOCK

WALLS COVERED
WITH HIGHLY
DECORATIVE FABRIC

ROMANESQUE-STYLE
ARCHITECTURAL
MOULDINGS AROUND
THE FIREPLACE, DOOR
AND WINDOW

HEATING FROM CAST-
IRON DUCTS IN THE
FLOOR

A BELL TO CALL THE
SERVANTS

DEEPLY CARVED
FURNITURE, STAINED
TO RESEMBLE EBONY

SUBSTANTIAL
PEDESTAL TABLE IN
THE CENTRE OF THE
ROOM

ECLECTICISM

CREATING THE STYLE

The many styles of decoration prevalent during the nineteenth century shared a common theme: a fascination with the past. It was a time of eclectic historicism on an unprecedented scale, including as it did, towards the middle of the century, forms of Gothic, neo-Rococo and Elizabethan. In 1851 the Great Exhibition of the Industry of All Nations was held in London's Crystal Palace and had on show any number of different historical styles on offer to the new, affluent middle classes. Manufacturers began producing vast quantities of furniture based on historical models to meet the new demand. What this means in terms of trying to recreate the style today is that you can use either authentic pieces of furniture from earlier periods or Victorian copies. What it also means is that there is still a good quantity of original Victorian pieces of furniture available in antiques stores and salerooms today.

There are two possible courses of action to take when creating this style. First, you can adhere to one particular style, such as Gothic, or, second, you can create an eclectic mixture of styles while ensuring that the themes are sympathetic. During the nineteenth century particular styles were used for specific rooms – for example, Louis Revival was often reserved for the bedroom, while 'Jacobethan' was preferred for hallways, dining-rooms and libraries – but there is no need to be too dogmatic today.

RICH, RED
UPHOLSTERY FOR THE
CHAIR COVERS

Richly sculpted marble firesurround from the second half of the nineteenth century, in Victoria Mansion, Maine.

ARCHITECTURAL ELEMENTS

*'Jacobethan' furniture epitomizes the
Victorian love for historical styles.*

FIREPLACES

The typical early Victorian fireplace is of a fairly simple, classically inspired design, often executed in marble; Gothic, 'Elizabethan' or Renaissance stylistic elements might also be in evidence. In general, drawing-room fireplaces should be in light-coloured marble, either white or dove grey; for the dining-room, black or black-and-yellow colour schemes are more typical. Alternative materials include other stones, painted wood and painted iron.

Coal, burned in a cast-iron grate, was the standard fuel in Britain during the nineteenth century, so basket grates are entirely appropriate.

Towards the middle of the century, following the Victorian penchant for draping everything in sight, fireplaces were often dressed in fabric. A flounced pelmet (cornice), perhaps of velvet, attached to the mantelshelf, and curtains that can be drawn across the opening when the fireplace is not in use would be in keeping. During the summer months, unused hearths can be filled with dried flowers.

STAIRCASES

The solid, carved newel post is a feature of early Victorian staircases. Handrails should ideally be of mahogany with either iron or carved-wood balustrading. Stairs should be fitted with a stair runner, with treads outside the carpeted area being painted a rich shade of dark brown.

DOORS AND WINDOWS

During the Victorian period, internal doors were usually four-panelled with plain mouldings. Whereas the trend during the Regency had favoured light woodwork, early Victorian doors were generally painted in a dark 'wood' colour. By contrast, in France and the United States the fashion was to forgo doors between reception rooms in favour of large-scale openings.

At the time, shapes of doors and windows

*A grand Victorian dining-room with
restrained curtain treatment.*

were used to express a number of architectural styles. There were rounded arches for the 'Italian' style and pointed, flattened arches for Gothic. One of the hallmarks of the Victorian façade was becoming established: the projecting, angled bay window, extending from ground level through one or two storeys.

After 1840, the manufacture of plate glass allowed new windows to be designed incorporating large panes. Also of great significance, the stained-glass revival was firmly underway.

*Sturdy cast-iron early Victorian
fireplace, c 1840*

*Marble fireplace with highly
decorative grate, c 1840*

Gothic-style woodwork in sombre colours.

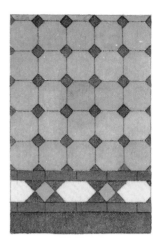

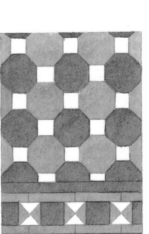

Cornice friezes with Gothic decoration

A series of designs for Victorian encaustic tiles, c 1840

DECORATIVE DETAILS

By the early years of the Victorian period, decorative architectural elements were almost entirely superficial, made of papier mâché and applied to the wall or ceiling surface rather than forming part of the built fabric. They are thus particularly easy to emulate in a period room. The ceilings should typically be flat, with a central decorative relief or rose from which the light fitting is suspended. A dado (wainscoting) or chair-rail is optional (they were often absent), but about three quarters of the way to the ceiling there should certainly be a picture-rail, to break up the expanse of the wall. Skirtingboards (baseboards) should be deep – up to 30 cm (12 in) high and about

4 cm (1½ in) thick – projecting out from the wall so that the wallpaper is protected from possible damage.

Early Victorian mouldings, friezes, cornices (crown moldings) and other decorations are often classical in spirit, although not as fine and elegant as those of the Georgian period; originally they were executed in plaster of Paris or papier mâché. 'Grecian' Classicism was popular in Europe and the United States until mid-century. This was also the period when eclecticism reached its peak, so that all sorts of other historical styles came into vogue. In Britain, there was some Gothic-style tracery, ribbing and moulded beams; later this was joined by the beginnings of

neo-Rococo, with its elaborate scrollwork and general richness of ornament. Technical advances gave rise to new stucco compositions which could be painted or papered over much more quickly and easily.

● Gothic revival architectural detail can be reflected on a small scale by the use of cornices and ceiling roses with 'lacy' detailing

FLOORS

Encaustic tiles, which had different coloured clays inlaid to form a pattern, began to be produced mechanically around 1840, and by 1850 were becoming the fashionable flooring for halls and porches. Similar plain, patterned and shaped floor tiles are still sold.

WALL COVERINGS AND FABRIC EFFECTS

High Victorian colour palette

ABOVE A High Victorian drawing-room.
TOP A particularly fine example of High Victorian wall painting.

WALLPAPER AND FABRIC

Wallpaper, first mass-produced in Britain in 1841, became the principal treatment for walls during this period and remained so for nearly a century.

In general, lighter papers should be adopted in the drawing-room and darker, richer papers in the dining-room.

Wallpapers imitating the effect of rich fabrics or simulated watered-silk paper depicting bunches of flowers tied with ribbons are appropriate. There are also Gothic designs to consider – flat, two-dimensional diaper or heraldic motifs – and patterns derived from Arabic or Moorish influence. Dark crimson flock paper will give a sombre, sumptuous look to a dining-room although it still suffers the disad-

vantage of being easily soiled; it can be typically set off with gilt moulding. Flock paper can also be used for bordering satin paper, which has a shiny finish. A multicoloured stencilled border would be a good touch.

At the lower end of the range, there are many simpler designs, including striped, spotted or sprigged motifs on plain backgrounds. Imitation marble or granite paper is appropriate for halls.

The entire wall except for the chair- and picture-rails could be papered from skirting (baseboard) to cornice (crown molding). Or you might create a false dado (wainscoting) by putting paper in a different pattern below the chair-rail. Originally, the most expensive paper would never have been applied below the dado level.

Although wallpaper gradually superseded other types of wall treatment, fabric remained an alternative until mid-century, after which time it could be afforded only by the very rich. Pale silk panels outlined in gilt mouldings reflect the style of well-to-do early Victorian drawing-rooms, as do leather panels embossed with gilt patterns. At the other end of the scale, simple printed cotton is a perfectly adequate and entirely appropriate form of wall covering.

● Wallpapers and fabrics printed or woven with flat, stylized Gothic patterns will immediately give a Gothic look; when more than one pattern is combined in a room scheme the fundamental richness of the style becomes apparent

PAINT

Ceilings can be tinted in shades to tone with the colour of the wallpaper. Grey and light green are typical, with more sombre colours such as deep crimson being used in dining-rooms. Cornices (crown moldings) should be left plain, not gilded or painted polychromatically; they might be in a slightly darker shade of the ceiling colour.

During the early Victorian period most woodwork reverted to the dark colours prevalent in the eighteenth century, either grained or painted a 'wood' shade. In Gothic rooms, the woodwork was often stained to simulate the effect of age.

SOFT FURNISHINGS

Light-coloured striped and floral chintz can be made into loose covers for drawing-rooms or bedrooms. Naturalistic pieces could be covered in plush, horsehair or dark silk, trimmed with floor-length fringing, gimp and tassels.

The Victorians displayed quantities of needlework, embroidered cloths, mats, antimacassars (originally used to protect seat upholstery from hair oil of that name), *petit point*, beadwork and, above all, Berlin woolwork. The craze for Berlin woolwork, a type of tapestry embroidery, lasted for the three decades following 1830. After the introduction of aniline and other chemical dyes, colours could be fairly lurid. Finished pieces can be incorporated into fire-screens, footstools, *prie-dieux* and chair-seats.

Bed curtains, if any, should be very similar to window treatments. Dressing-tables can be lavishly draped in lace-covered calico.

WINDOW TREATMENTS

After 1830 window treatments became symmetrical once more. Divided curtains, looped back low down and trailing onto the floor, would emulate a typical effect; contrasting linings or corded edges would give added authenticity. Behind the heavy main curtains should be a pair of sub-curtains in lace or muslin.

At the time, the entire window was usually framed by a deep flat pelmet or lambrequin, which extended down one-

This hallway shows strong nineteenth-century Gothic elements particularly in the shape of the door frame.

third of the curtain at the centre and almost to the floor at either side. The lambrequin might be elaborately shaped and trimmed to reflect a particular style, such as Gothic or Moorish.

A window might also have decorative roller blinds – painted, printed, woven, fringed or embroidered. During this period, there were also 'glass curtains' (like net curtains) which hung against the lower panes to preserve privacy.

Heavy silk or worsted damask, figured satin or merino are the fabrics to be favoured for drawing-rooms, with muslin for the summer. Green or red damask suits the formality of dining-rooms. Chintz should be reserved mainly for loose covers and for bedroom drapery. Trellis, floral sprigs and bouquets are in keeping, as would be any design evocative of Gothic tracery or Islamic motifs.

● At a window you could use either heavy fringed drapery, pulled back to one side with twisted rope, or divided curtains with a solid pelmet shaped into a Gothic form

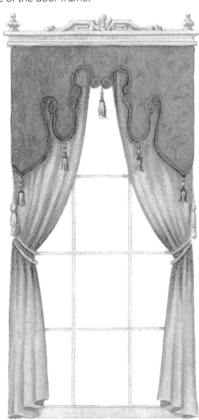

Window treatment, c 1850

THE VICTORIAN AGE
CREATING THE STYLE: ECLECTICISM

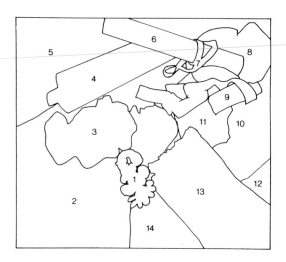

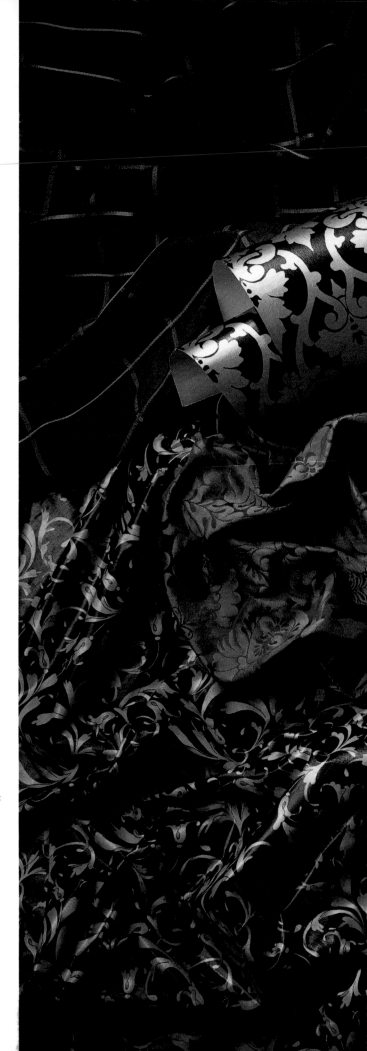

1 gilt embrasse; 2 glazed cotton; 3 silk damask; 4 screen-printed wallpaper; 5 plaid; 6 hand-printed wallpaper; 7 antique trimming; 8 damask; 9 antique trimming; 10 woven 'needlepoint' fabric; 11 woven 'needlepoint' fabric; 12 striped damask; 13 antique silk damask cushion; 14 moire-effect linen.

Features from almost every historical period were combined in the first half of the nineteenth century, with Medieval, Renaissance and Baroque styles enjoying particular favour towards the middle of the century. Wallpapers and fabrics were printed with Gothic, heraldic and Moorish designs, among others. Lighter papers, with ribbons or bunches of flowers, adorned bedrooms and drawing-rooms, with darker, richer papers being reserved for dining-rooms, hallways and studies. Curtains and door treatments tended to be symmetrical, using sumptuous brocades, velvets, tartans or damasks, heavily trimmed with fringes and often lined with a contrasting colour. Lighter touches were achieved with chintz, most often kept for bedrooms or used for loose covers.

FURNITURE AND FITTINGS

ROOM ARRANGEMENT

The beginning of the Victorian era saw rooms become firmly assigned to specific functions. As well as a separation of activities, there was increased segregation of children into nurseries and servants into servants' quarters, wings or 'below stairs' offices. In general, the drawing-room was regarded as having a 'feminine' nature, and was decorated and furnished accordingly; the dining-room, with its air of sober formality, was 'masculine'.

To be in style, the layout of your furniture should be fixed in informal conversational groupings, with the fireplace as the main focal point. The emphasis is on comfort and domesticity, with the hearth the symbolic centre of home life, a place to display memorabilia and all types of personal treasures.

The windows of the time, with their increasingly heavy drapery, brought less natural light into rooms and so no longer competed as focal points for furniture. The move away from the window was also promoted by improvements in illumination: oil lighting was now much more reliable and later, of course, gas lighting became commonly available.

- For a Scottish baronial look, use a tartan in a single traditional pattern or plaid fabric throughout a room
- Other suitable fabrics are velvets, damasks in deep reds and greens and brocades, all heavily fringed or used in deep-buttoned upholstery
- Decorative objects that distinguish the style include coats of arms, sporting prints, guns and armorial objects, antlers and horn accessories.

TYPES OF FURNITURE

In the 1840s there was a wide variety of furniture styles from which to choose. A heavier version of the Greek Classicism of Thomas Hope was popular for 'masculine' furniture – that is, pieces for studies and dining-rooms. Neo-Rococo was fashionable for equipping the 'feminine' drawing-room, boudoir and bedroom, while halls

Tartan, used for chairs, curtains and an elaborate pelmet, combine with a deep red carpet and hunting memorabilia to create a study in true 'Scottish baronial' style.

might be given an 'Elizabethan' flavour. (Much of what Victorians termed 'Tudor' or 'Elizabethan' was in fact Stuart.) Interestingly enough, there was a vogue for collecting antiques and for making up pieces that incorporated old carving.

The Gothic movement gave rise to a revolutionary style of furniture which displayed, rather than artfully concealed, its method of construction. But Gothic furniture was by and large uncomfortable and so not very popular – unlike today.

Much more successful at the time were Naturalistic designs, curvaceous, comfortable pieces which lent themselves to an excess of trimming and decoration. It is the carving on such furniture which is 'naturalistic', featuring flowers and leaves, but a

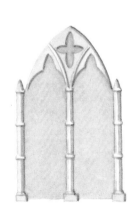

more distinctive characteristic is the upholstered shape. The 'overstuffed' appearance of Victorian upholstery, together with the new fashion for deep-buttoning, marked a new era for comfort and informality. Typical Naturalistic pieces, therefore, include the circular sofa, the ottoman, the pouffe, the sinuous *vis à vis* and the *crapaud*, a deep-buttoned easy chair. Drawing-rooms sometimes include a *prie-dieu*, upholstered in needlework and carved in the Elizabethan style.

Furniture for the drawing-room was often sold in suites, which comprised a sofa, a pair of armchairs and a set of upright or balloon-backed chairs. Should you wish to create a drawing-room in this style, you might also look out for a circular or loo table, card- and sewing-tables, display cabinets and whatnots.

Dining-room furniture is more massive. There could be a sideboard or a chiffonier, which consists of a top with display shelves and a lower part with latticed doors. Dining-tables are generally of the pedestal variety, sometimes with extensions. A marble-topped table is a feature of the hall, along with a mahogany hat-stand.

By mid-century metal beds, in either cast iron or brass, superseded the four-poster or tester bed. Other bedroom furniture includes wardrobes, chests of drawers and wash-stands.

Mahogany was still a common material during the nineteenth century, although the more expensive walnut was often preferred for dining-room pieces. Rosewood, sandalwood and satinwood were other luxury materials. Papier mâché was used to make Rococo-style boxes, trays, firescreens and occasional tables and chairs, as well as larger items. It could be japanned and decorated to simulate mother-of-pearl inlay. Simple cane furniture, which is easily obtainable today, can be used for conservatories and terraces.

LIGHTING

In 1845 paraffin (kerosene) replaced colza oil for lighting, which meant illumination became easier and more dependable. Crystal fittings would be appropriate for a main room; elsewhere brass, copper and bronze are more common. Table-lamps, wall-brackets and hanging devices – in styles originally designed for use with oil lighting – should all feature in an early Victorian scheme. However, candles were still the most important means of lighting, so it would not be out of keeping to use them.

DECORATIVE OBJECTS

Rooms can acquire a private and more personal atmosphere, typical of early Victorian interiors, with the display of memorabilia and souvenirs. Miniatures and silhouettes can be hung in groups around the fireplace. The mantelshelf may be cluttered with figures, vases and crystal, all arranged symmetrically around an important centrepiece such as an elaborate clock in a domed case.

CARPETS

Patterns should be essentially floral, possibly featuring full-blown cabbage roses and acanthus leaves. Suitable colours include dark green, scarlet and combinations of pink and white.

Although, to be in period, you should fit carpeting wall-to-wall in the dining-room, you should leave a margin of floor around the perimeter of the drawing-room carpet. This area was originally covered with oil-cloth, linen or drugget but today it is just as effective simply to paint it a dark colour to blend in with the skirtings (baseboards). Similarly, in the hall, you should grain the floor surrounds to match the skirting boards and paint the stair-treads, where not covered by carpet, a dark colour.

A Victorian-style bedroom can be left uncarpeted, the boards only covered by a mitred strip around the bed and a mat in front of the dressing-table.

As ever, oilcloths were a popular cheap alternative to carpet. They were widely adopted in hallways and were also used to protect valuable carpets. Should you want to include oilcloths in your scheme, they could simulate mosaic pavements or could be decorated in Greek key patterns. Standard colours are sombre shades of dark brown and green. Other alternatives to carpet include hand-made hooked, plaited or rag rugs, plaited felt and split-cane or rattan matting.

KITCHEN AND BATHROOM FITTINGS

The development of the cast-iron range revolutionized popular domestic cooking arrangements. These early stoves consist of an open-fire grate with ovens on either side. Such stoves are available today, but their use will be largely decorative.

Even by mid-century lavatories were still only for the wealthy; in North America bathrooms were much more common. There was, however, a washstand in every bedroom, with two in a double bedroom. These consisted of a wooden frame in which was set a marble top, holding one or two basins, and a tile splashback.

A series of chair-backs, demonstrating the variety of styles favoured in the first half of the nineteenth century. Caned panels. Gothic tracery, barley sugar twists and deeply-buttoned leather were among the most popular adornments

RECREATION OF A
CLUTTERED HIGH
VICTORIAN PARLOUR

WALLPAPER WITH A
LOUD FLORAL DESIGN

DEEP MAROON
VELVET DRAPES FOR
WINDOWS AND
FIREPLACE

TASSELS AND
TRIMMINGS TO
MATCH

THIN SHADES
BENEATH AN ORNATE
WINDOW
TREATMENT

CIRCULAR SIDE-TABLE
COVERED WITH
FABRIC AND A
MULTITUDE OF
OBJECTS

A PEDESTAL TO
DISPLAY PLANTS OR
ORNAMENTS

PORTRAIT BUSTS AND
PORCELAIN
ORNAMENTS

GAS WALL FITTINGS
AND OIL TABLE LAMPS

132

HIGH VICTORIAN

CREATING THE STYLE

During the second half of the nineteenth century a 'comfortable' upholstered style emerged which drew on many historical themes and which depended for its effect on a multitude of accessories. The style was widely popular throughout Europe and the United States as well as in Australia.

At the time, outward 'show' – the need to be *seen* to be prosperous – meant that rooms became thoroughly overcrowded: potted palms jostled with whatnots, *étagères* and folding screens, Chesterfield sofas, spoon-backed chairs, deep leather armchairs, pianos, plant-stands and sculptures on plinths. Ornaments covered every surface, and tables – even overmantels – might be covered by heavy fabric in dark, rich colours.

One of the most appealing aspects of this style is its comfortable synthesis of disparate elements. However, the effect does rely on a mass of accessories, so it may take some time to collect sufficient objects for a successful scheme. Moreover, to many people the overcrowded effect can be oppressive: rather nice to look at, but not so nice to live in.

CAST-IRON FIREPLACE
COMPLETE WITH
KETTLE STAND

Upright piano in a richly decorated corner of Thomas Carlyle's celebrated house in London.

ARCHITECTURAL ELEMENTS

*The landscape painted on the frieze of this Arkansas dining-room
demonstrates the importance of decoration in the nineteenth century.*

*A tiled floor in the popular colours of
black, white, terracotta, stone and slate.*

FIREPLACES

The fireplace of a main room should ideally be of plain, polished white marble, with carved corbels or brackets supporting a mantelshelf. Cement or plaster designs are correct for smaller rooms. During the late Victorian period fireplaces came in a variety of styles, but many were 'after Adam', in keeping with the general fascination for eighteenth-century decoration.

Technical innovations resulted in modifications to the design of grates. The arched or rectangular 'register' grate had at the opening to the chimney a door that could be used to regulate the air-flow. Later, grates were shallower, with inclined backs, splayed sides and an 'economiser'. This gadget helped to keep the fire burning steadily but not too quickly. Grates were often decorated with classical motifs.

DECORATIVE DETAILS

Fibrous plaster gradually replaced papier mâché for wall and ceiling decorations. A cornice (crown molding), in low plaster relief, and a ceiling rose (medallion), which could have a floral or leaf design, would be in keeping.

Picture-rails are standard and chair-rails almost so. Decorative mouldings could be used to form panels for a grander scheme.

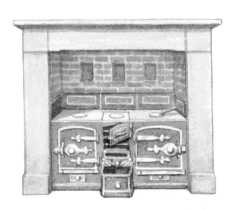

*Cast-iron range of the type found in
many kitchens, c 1850*

*Simple but elegant cast-iron grate,
c 1865*

*Fire-surround with painted ceramic
tiles and brass fender, c 1870*

STAIRCASES

Late Victorian staircases were of heavy design; wooden ones should be painted brown or grained and varnished. The newel post should be substantial and balusters should be turned.

DOORS AND WINDOWS

Interior doors were generally four-panelled and usually painted in a dark colour (not stripped). The front door was often rather elaborate, with panels of patterned stained glass.

The most common window design during this period was the sash with large single panes. The angled bay window at the front of the house and French windows at the rear were common features.

Stained glass can be used in windows, chiefly those in hallways or on staircases.

FLOORS

Encaustic tiles can be found in many late Victorian halls, porches and terraces. If you are lucky enough to find some in an antique shop, lay them in 'medieval' patterns.

● For entrance halls, porches, kitchens and utility rooms a tiled floor is a durable and attractive solution: occasionally, original encaustic floor tiles are obtainable but reproductions are now available also

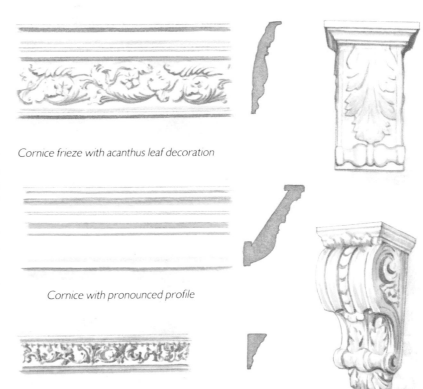

Cornice frieze with acanthus leaf decoration

Cornice with pronounced profile

Cornice frieze with floral decoration

A series of brackets, complete with acanthus leaf decoration, scrolls and a head. These brackets are usually to be found in hallways, sometimes supporting arches

A selection of ceiling roses (medallions) showing delicate plaster work typical of the 1880s

WALL COVERINGS AND FABRIC EFFECTS

WALLPAPER

In 1877 the first commercially produced relief paper came onto the market. This was Lincrusta, which was long-lasting, scrubbable and available in a range of designs imitating wood, plaster or leather. Anaglypta, a slightly later invention, was similar but lighter, cheaper and more flexible. Still available today, both types can be painted or varnished and will work well as a tough decorative solution for dados (wainscoting), particularly in halls and dining-rooms. Lincrusta can also be applied to ceilings.

The area of wall above the dado can be covered with a 'filling' paper, which might be patterned with dense, organic designs (such as scrollwork and acanthus) in dark, saturated colours. Alternatively, reproduction tapestry papers could be used in a dining-room. Thinner, lighter papers in chintz-type designs are more suitable for a bedroom, while Japanese grass paper might feature in a drawing-room. Interestingly, during this period the first nursery papers appeared; they were patterned with characters and scenes from popular books.

PAINT

Except for the frieze (the area between picture-rail and cornice (crown molding)), which became much deeper and more elaborate during the late Victorian period when it was often adorned with distinctive painted or stencilled designs, paint should be very rarely used as a wall treatment.

However, ceilings should be painted. Cream, stone and dull pastels are more suitable than white. Skirting (base boards), chair- and picture-rails should be a dark 'wood' colour, grained or varnished.

● All woodwork should be grained a dark colour: this may seem a drastic step, but it is a relatively inexpensive authentic detail

TILES

The late nineteenth century saw the rise of the use of tiles, particularly in rooms where hygiene was important such as kitchens and bathrooms, with encaustic tiles being especially popular for hall floors. Tiles with relief mouldings were decorated with majolica glazes.

High Victorian colour palette

This Arkansas drawing-room has a stunning ceiling as well as an elaborate parquet floor.

This fine set of portières *demonstrates the important rôle of Victorian drapery.*

SOFT FURNISHINGS

Deep-buttoning went largely out of fashion by the 1880s. However, chairs and sofas should be heavily stuffed, covered with velvet upholstery and trimmed with fringes. Trimmings were an important element of the scheme. Stamped leather or tapestry would be suitable coverings for the seats of dining-chairs.

Seasonal variations can be introduced by the use of loose covers in chintz or cretonne (a thick, printed cotton). In the late nineteenth century aniline dyes produced intense colours, and patterns were generally floral – full-blown roses, hydrangeas, lilies and chrysanthemums. Muslin and lace antimacassars, as well as scarves and festoons of drapery between chair-legs, can complete the somewhat 'overdressed' look.

WINDOW TREATMENTS

The late Victorian interior was a gloomy place. Almost all natural light was excluded by layers of drapery. The main set of curtains, used for winter, should be dark, fringed, tasselled velvet or brocade, covered with an elaborate pelmet (cornice) or valance. 'Continued drapery', where a

series of windows along one wall is unified by a single pelmet, is an option should you have such a series of windows. Beneath the main set of curtains should be sub-curtains of lace or muslin; alternatively, you could have net festoons with scalloped edges. Beneath the sub-curtains put roller blinds, which can be used on their own for lesser rooms, in the kitchen, for example.

In the summer the heavy velvet curtains should be taken down (partly because they fade in the sunshine). Leave the sub-curtains, but substitute something lighter – perhaps chintz or cotton hangings – as an alternative to the main ones.

DRAPERY

Windows were not the only curtained features during the second half of the nineteenth century. The average Victorian drawing-room offers more than half a dozen different places for drapery including fireplaces, alcoves, mirrors, cupboards and doors. *Portières* – curtains and pelmets (cornices) – could be used for every door, if desired. The chimney can be swathed in swagged pelmets and draw-curtains or draped in dark fringed plush. Other possible applications are on picture frames, pots and *jardinières*. Japanese scarves can be used for 'artistic' tie-backs.

With such an emphasis on drapery, it was natural that bed-hangings should return to favour. In a concession to hygiene, the half-canopy was more common than the full tester. Cretonne and dotted and plain Swiss are suitable fabrics for this type of treatment and are all readily available.

• For a simple window treatment hang patterned Nottingham lace and madras muslin curtains fixed beneath an elaborate covered pelmet trimmed with fringes, tassels, braids and twisted ropes
• To give the effect of a Victorian draped mantelshelf, simply attach an elaborate fringe around the edge of a stiff fabric pelmet (which could even coordinate with other furniture trimmings on furnishings and curtains; make sure that this will not constitute a fire hazard)

Heavy door curtains, complete with pelmet, c 1870

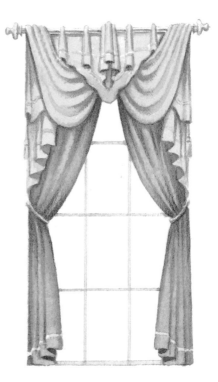

A particularly flamboyant door treatment. c 1885

THE VICTORIAN AGE
CREATING THE STYLE: HIGH VICTORIAN

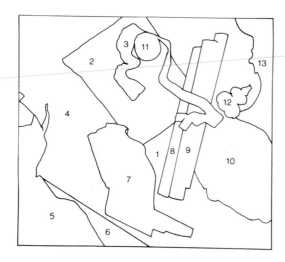

1 cotton chintz; 2 antique paisley cushion; 3 fringe; 4 glazed cotton; 5 printed cotton; 6 painted Anaglypta; 7 wallpaper border; 8 hand-printed wallpaper; 9 hand-printed wallpaper; 10 glazed cotton; 11 braid trimming; 12 finial; 13 antique lace curtain.

The image most readily associated with High Victorian style is one of dense patterns and fabric covering almost every surface. Anaglypta in sombre colours contrasted with wallpaper in vivid, full-blown floral designs. Curtain treatments were elaborate using heavy swags of carefully arranged silk velvet or worsted fabric over simple sun blinds or muslin undercurtains. Delicate lace was also hung at windows to great effect. Heavily stuffed seat furniture was covered in velvet, leather or needlework and embellished with heavy fringes. In summer, these covers were often exchanged for lighter loose covers in glazed chintz or cretonne. The overwhelming effect was emphasized by scarves and shawls draped across every available piece of furniture, from chairs and tables to plant-stands and bookcases.

FURNITURE AND FITTINGS

ROOM ARRANGEMENT

High Victorian rooms were unquestionably fussy and cluttered. Recreating the style exactly might produce a result that seems oppressive and claustrophobic to modern eyes. In the drawing-room there should be no centre table; instead, use plenty of occasional tables, each laden with a cargo of objects, framed photographs and curios. Whatnots, display cabinets, screens, shelves and plant-stands should also feature. A 'cosy corner' could be created by partitioning a section of the room with a screen draped with exotic shawls.

The dining-room should still be formal in layout and 'masculine' in general mood, filled with massive furniture and dominated by a heavy pedestal table.

At the time, male preserves included the study (often fairly Gothic in flavour), the smoking-room and, in wealthier households, the billiard-room. The latter were typically rather rakish retreats, with divans for lounging and Moorish- or Turkish-style decoration. It is unlikely that you will have enough room to allocate space for these various specific purposes, but certainly you can aim to create something of the effect in a den or study.

ABOVE An inspired recreation of a cluttered High Victorian bedroom.

BELOW Neo-Rococo chairs manufactured in the nineteenth century.

TYPES OF FURNITURE

Furniture was very varied during this period, in terms of both style and quality. There was a general return to the late eighteenth century for inspiration. At the top end of the market there were some extremely skilful copies of Louis XVI, Chippendale, Hepplewhite and Sheraton, almost indistinguishable from the real thing. At the lower end of the market, there was a whole range of badly produced and heavily proportioned French-style furniture, coarsely carved and skimpily made. The fall in standards resulting from such mass production was responsible for the popularity of antiques among the rich. As an alternative to the antique 'look', there was a wealth of simpler 'cottage' furniture to choose from.

The neo-Louis look was promoted in France by the Empress Eugénie, who cultivated the decorative style of Marie Antoinette. In the United States, this style was known as neo-Grec; commercially, it became the 'Style Rothschild' or 'Style Ritz', typical of grand hotels. Much of the furniture was in mahogany and satinwood.

There was a variety of styles and a mixture was considered more tasteful than

Louis XIV-style chair, with tapestry upholstery and giltwood frame

Louis V-style chair, with gold-embroidered upholstery and painted frame

Louis XVI-style chair, with silk upholstery and giltwood frame

a room furnished all in one type. Japan (or 'art') furniture was one of the most significant; pieces in this style are thin-legged and generally spindly, and have gilt decoration on a black ground. Bamboo – particularly for small tables and plant-stands – would be a fitting expression of the Japanese style.

Furniture in the 'Renaissance' style was often adopted for the dining-room; Moorish style was common in smoking- and billiard-rooms. Bedrooms were furnished in suites of 'Adam' furniture, often painted white to emphasize its hygienic qualities. Beds were still chiefly of brass or iron. Built-in cupboards were becoming common, especially in bedrooms.

● For special occasions create a Victorian mood with a dining-room table highly decorated with flowers, fruit and elaborate candlesticks

● Transform a sofa or an armchair by covering it with a paisley shawl, an embroidered throw or even an oriental rug or kelim, then add cushions

LIGHTING
With the invention of the incandescent mantle in 1887, gas became the main domestic light source. More and more homes were fitted with gas brackets throughout; Rise-and-fall 'gasoliers' were common ceiling fittings. The selection of reproduction Victorian fittings increases daily, so you should have no difficulty in finding something to suit your scheme.

DECORATIVE OBJECTS
To capture the feeling of a late Victorian interior your room should be overflowing with plants and incidental objects of all description. The Japanese influence is important. If you can get hold of brass trays and little tables, perhaps inlaid with mother-of-pearl, so much the better; these were examples of native crafts brought back from far-flung corners of the Empire. Flat surfaces can be covered with such items as vases of peacock feathers, wax fruit, dried grasses and framed photographs.

Walls can be covered with gilt-framed pictures. Typical of the early Victorian style, you could have an elaborate overmantel with shelves and niches to take yet more objects and photographs.

CARPETS
In the 1880s fitted carpets all but disappeared. The preoccupation with hygiene led to the prevalence of stained floor-boards (often oak) or parquet, with Turkish or Persian carpets, Brussels or Axminster squares, or rugs. Animal skins on top of rugs were very fashionable.

A new product, linoleum, replaced oil-cloth as the preferred cheap alternative to carpet. Linoleum is currently enjoying a revival and, consequently, there is a vast choice of suitable colours and patterns. Matting was popular during the second half of the nineteenth century, and is another cheap alternative today.

KITCHEN AND BATHROOM FITTINGS
After 1870 upper floors began to be plumbed with running water. There were new cast-iron wash-stands and baths, with decorative feet and ornate patterns. Toilets

This bathroom is a masterpiece of the Victorian tiler's art.

had cast-iron frames, mahogany lids and decorative porcelain bowls. There were few indoor lavatories.

In the bigger towns, kitchens too were plumbed with water. Gadgets, such as mangles and mincers, came into common use.

A fine selection of Victorian gas lamps

GIVE · DO · US · EACH · DAY · OUR · DAILY · BREAD

CRAFTSMANSHIP AND DESIGN

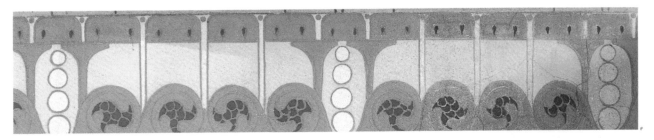

Detail of a cabinet designed by Philip Webb, c 1865 at Morris's Red House.

The confused mixture of eclecticism with opulence and mass-production with intricate handicrafts and applied decoration during the latter half of the nineteenth century created, in the last 25 years or so of the century, some radical reactions. After decades of slavishly following earlier styles, the need for expression of individuality asserted itself. This was manifested in more personal styles of interior decoration, in an appreciation of individually crafted objects and of the simpler decoration that still existed in rural areas. Since the essence of these traditional styles was function, it could be argued that this reform in taste heralded the eventual emergence of the Modern movement in the following century.

Medieval-inspired decoration on a tile designed by William de Morgan.

A fireplace at Little Holland House, the home that Frank Dickinson built for himself at Carshalton, Surrey, in 1910.

THE AESTHETIC MOVEMENT

*A turn-of-the-century interior painted by
L Campbell-Taylor.*

*A house in Bedford Park, London, with tiles
by William de Morgan.*

In 1868 Charles Eastlake published his book *Hints on Household Taste*, in which he frequently used the term 'aesthetic' to refer to lighter, less eclectic styles. He emphasized the personal element that should be found in home decoration and expanded on the tradition of handicrafts in medieval England, rejecting mass-produced furniture in favour of individually made pieces. Sensibly, he decreed that each home should be an individual work of art, assembled slowly and lovingly rather than thrown together as quickly as possible in one go.

Taking its cue from Eastlake, the Aesthetic movement was born, although its widespread effect on interior decoration was not felt until the 1890s. The two main styles that embodied the principles of this movement were Queen Anne and Japanese (see page 121). One of the prime movers in the reassessment of Japanese Art was Arthur Lasenby Liberty (1843–1917), the founder of Liberty of Regent Street, London, who had formerly been the Oriental manager of a London importing company. Importers' and dealers' showrooms and Liberty's store became favourite meeting places for the artistic élite. One of the leading dealers of the day, Murray Marks, proved the connection between the decline in taste for the Gothic and the new Aesthetic fashion by getting Richard Norman Shaw to redesign his shop in the style, using an unusual (for then) creamy colour for the woodwork.

Symbols of the cult for Japan, for art decoration and for its attendant aestheticism turned up everywhere. There were the stylized sunflowers on the gables of Lowther Lodge (now the Royal Geographical Society building) in Kensington Gate, London. There was the famous Peacock Room (now in the Freer Museum in Washington DC) painted by James McNeill Whistler for a shipping magnate, Frederick Leyland, and originally designed by the architect and designer Thomas Jeckyll (1827–1881), who was one of the first to design furniture inspired by Japan. There was also the Liberty of London peacock symbol and, of course, the lily, which became a kind of signature in itself of a movement personified by Oscar Wilde and Whistler – not to mention an easy target for lampooners. Gilbert and Sullivan's operatic skit on Oriental mania, *The*

Art Nouveau and Aesthetic styles are reflected in this Viennese dining-room, painted by K Zajicek in 1911.

Mikado, and their caricature of Oscar Wilde in *Patience* parodied the sentimental passion of vegetable fashion (a forerunner of Art Nouveau). This was followed by Gerald du Maurier's poem 'Oscar', first published in *Punch*, which described the typical Japanese-loving aesthete as 'quite too consummately utter, as well as too utterly quiet'.

Max Beerbohm once called E W Godwin (1833–1886), who, in conjunction with Whistler, produced many beautiful rooms in which structure was simplified to its essential elements and decoration limited to a minimum, 'the greatest aesthetic of them all'. One of the interiors designed by Godwin was for the house that

Oscar Wilde leased in Tite Street, Chelsea. Decorated in white and grey, it was a precursor of the 1930s white-on-white style of Syrie Maugham (1879–1955).

The quietness of Godwin's colour scheme was innovative, since most of the colours of the time were very sharp and included a great deal of yellow. His own scheme for Lord Limerick's Dromere Castle in County Limerick, Ireland, was exotically extravagant by comparison. In the drawing-room, for example, was Oriental-inspired furniture (designed, of course, by Godwin himself) ebonized and upholstered in yellow satin and set against walls washed in blue and green; the dark, boarded ceiling was decorated with Celtic scrolls.

THE ARTS AND CRAFTS MOVEMENT

The Arts and Crafts movement evolved partly out of a concern for the British working man (or the BWM) who, because of mechanized techniques and the seemingly insatiable thirst of the affluent middle classes for new styles, was being palmed off with mass-produced mediocrity. Another factor in the movement's development was sympathy for the individual craftsman's desire for isolated production; yet another was a belief in the need for stylistic unity in architecture and decoration. This last concern was the movement's most important contribution to the development of interior decoration.

The architects C R Ashbee (1863–1942) and W R Lethaby (1857–1931) were the founders and leaders of the Arts and Crafts movement; other powerful exponents were the poet and artist William Morris (see page 120), the architect and designer C F A Voysey (1857–1941) and the cabinet-makers Ernest Gimson (1864–1919) and the Barnsley brothers, Ernest (1861–1926) and Sidney (1863–1926). The movement gained cohesion through its allegiance to the writings of John Ruskin (1819–1900), who advocated a medieval guild system. Ruskin himself donated £7,000 towards the foundation of the first modern guild, the Guild of St George. This was followed by a series of groups and societies that formed and regrouped, until by a little after the turn of the century there were similar guilds operating throughout Britain the United States, and Europe. Ashbee's own Guild of Handicrafts at one time numbered about 150 working men, women and boys.

In terms of architecture the style is foreshadowed in the family house that William Morris asked Philip Webb to design for him. The now-famous Red House, at Bexleyheath (1859), is the result of Webb's search for a modern, ahistorical style. With its asymmetry, exposed brick fireplaces, unrelieved woodwork and idiosyncratic unpretentious furnishings, it set the pattern for the classic English suburban and country home of the early twentieth century.

As a result of their interest in the forms and techniques of traditional country furniture and in the time-honoured woodworking skills, the furniture that Morris's colleagues produced generally featured the

Standen, Sussex, built by Philip Webb in 1894. Webb decorated the house with Morris's wallpapers and textiles.

structural elements: mortise-and-tenon joints, dovetails and pegs were all emphasized as part of the exterior design. Good old honest oak, previously the preserve of country carpenters and the neo-Gothic (which undoubtedly influenced the Arts and Crafts movement), predominated. Carving was kept to a minimum and few elements were machine-turned, instead being generally faceted or chamfered. Metal fittings were likewise exposed, becoming one of the few forms of permissible ornament: copper strap-hinges, drawer- and door-handles and upholstery tacks were common features. Chair-seats tended to be rush-bottomed or, if covered, more often with leather than with fabric.

Shops such as Liberty and Heals were responsible for the fact that large numbers of people accepted these simple styles; they promoted the notion that the use of a few well designed pieces of furniture was preferable to the use of a host of ugly items. However, the success of these and other stores was probably due to the fact that the furniture they sold tended to be a little more elaborate than that produced by Morris, decorated with repoussé (raised-relief) copper panels and inlaid with fruitwood or mother-of-pearl.

Worship of anything homespun and hand-crafted created a boom in the production of embroideries and textiles. Amateurs and professionals made lacework, coverlets, tablecloths, runners, screens, firescreens and tapestries. The designs produced by Morris and Co. resembled those of their fabrics and wallpaper, and stylized flowers and plants abounded in the various British design schools. In the United States, embroidery schools sprang up everywhere; their designs derived from Colonial patterns or from Morris's motifs.

Hand-loom weaving was revived in Britain in 1883, possibly in reaction to the mechanized Jacquard loom and the intricate patterns it produced. Morris, Edward Burne-Jones (1833–1898) and Walter Crane (1845–1915) produced fabrics, and elsewhere in Britain silk damasks and brocades were woven. In the United States rag rugs and imitations of Indian blankets were produced in large amounts and were extremely popular.

The 'artistic' interior used lighter colours than previously. A shade of dull green became especially prevalent, replacing the varnished mahogany that had been used for skirting (baseboards), door-cases and chair-rails, and provided an excellent background for the fashionable William Morris and Walter Crane wallpapers and fabrics.

By this time a low dado panel (wainscoting) generally covered the walls between the skirting board (baseboard) and the chair-rail (used since the eighteenth century to prevent chairs from damaging the walls). The wall above the dado was covered with paper, bordered at its top edge by a picture-rail which could be deepened at will to support oriental fans, plates or a collection of blue-and-white porcelain. Other contemporary ornaments stressed simplicity: there were copper and pewter lamps, vases and candlesticks and salt-glazed stoneware, pottery and ceramics.

The movement's gentle 'home-owner aesthetic' was well caught by the architect Halsey Ricardo:

Until the house, until the room, has been lived in, all looks inhuman, forbidding; it is only when the walls and their contents are redolent of human attention and human care that the interior and its furniture can be a pride to its owner and a joy to those who see and use them.

Little Holland House, built in Surrey in 1910 by its owner, Frank Dickinson.

Wall paintings and a typical Arts and Crafts fireplace in the bedroom of Little Holland House.

ARTS AND CRAFTS AND AMERICAN STYLE

Mission style originated in California when the congregation of a Franciscan mission church in San Francisco, unable to afford furnishings for the church, started to make their own chairs to replace the pews. A decorator, Dora Martin, saw them and was so impressed with their style that she sent a model – a simple, rush-seated chair – to Joseph McHugh, a furniture manufacturer in New York City. McHugh reproduced the line in fumed or smoked ash (later in fumed oak) with little decoration save whittled leg-ends, and sold the results through his Popular Shop. And popular they did indeed become.

The most respected producer of this style was Gustav Stickley (1857–1942). He spent his youth helping out in his uncle's chair shop and then, in 1898, travelled to Europe. By the time he returned he was a disciple of Morris and an admirer of Ruskin. Stickley founded his Craftsman Workshops, which took up the Mission style. His magazine *The Craftsman*, which became the mouthpiece for American Arts and Crafts between 1901 and 1916, gave its name to his style of architecture and interior design, of which Mission style was an important part. Craftsman furniture, made of oak with a strong, straight rectilinear design and rush- or leather-seated, became so popular that it was distributed throughout the United States.

The other exponents of the style were the members of the Roycroft Community, whose founder was Elbert Hubbard (1856–1915), the publisher of the magazine *Philistine*. Roycroft furniture was usually made from oak, although sometimes ash and mahogany were used; it was plain, with prominent mortise-and-tenon joints and tapering legs ending in rounded feet.

Two of the greatest figures in American interior decoration at this time were Louis Comfort Tiffany (1848–1933) and Frank Lloyd Wright (1869–1959). The company L C Tiffany produced finely crafted furniture and decoration which were frequently of Moorish or Japanese flavour; it was known also for its stained glass, its iridescent glass and pottery and its ceramics. At the Columbian Exposition held in 1893 in Chicago, Tiffany's magical glass-making reached glorious heights in a modern Byzantine chapel made from more than a million minute pieces of iridescent,

ABOVE *Arts and Crafts furniture made by Henry M. and Charles S. Greene of Pasadena, California*
LEFT *A typical early twentieth-century summer house in East Hampton, Long Island.*

opaline glass, with 12 stained-glass windows and a sanctuary lamp made of glass inset with jewels. His works were very influential.

The antithesis of Tiffany was Frank Lloyd Wright, who helped to bring Arts and Crafts to Chicago in the 1890s. He and the other designers who adopted the so-called Prairie School style used a clean, geometric design in architecture, furniture, carpets and stained glass. Their architecture followed the dicta of Louis Sullivan (1856–1924) that the outward form of a building should express its function and that construction materials should form part of the design idiom. The simple rectilinearity of Wright's furniture deliberately suited machine-production (unlike many other Arts and Crafts designs): Wright abhorred machines only when they were used to perform 'non-mechanical' tasks, such as carving.

*Gustav Stickley furniture and contemporary textiles were used in this recreation
of an Arts and Crafts interior. Strong colour on the walls complements
the sturdy wooden furniture.*

ART NOUVEAU

Samuel Bing (1838–1905), a French dealer in Oriental art who was visiting the Columbian Exposition, was particularly impressed by Tiffany's work, especially his leaded glass lamps and special iridescent and freely shaped Favrile glass, sometimes combined with bronze-like alloys and other metals. Bing returned to Paris and, in 1895, opened a shop called *Salon de l'Art Nouveau*, where he made a prominent display of Tiffany's glass. The shop became famous and gave its name to a new style. The epitome of a novel escapist mood, the style was characterized by extravagant sinuous ornament based on organic forms drawn from nature, and was unique in having little historical connection. Although the Art Nouveau period lasted only a very short time (roughly 1892 to the early 1900s), the style has remained influential to the present day.

A Belgian, Victor Horta (1861–1947), was one of the style's first exponents. Horta was both an architect and a decorator, and he designed most of his interiors and exteriors in the grand tradition. Like the great French nineteenth-century neo-Gothic architect and apologist, Eugène Viollet-le-Duc, Horta became extremely interested in the structural and decorative possibilities of the use of iron in architecture, and in the strength and power the metal could imply through even the most delicate forms. His sinuous exposed ironwork, his famous curving staircases with their tendril-like balustrades (repeated in patterns on floors, walls and ceilings) and his flowing lines in wall panelling, plaster-work and furnishing (inserted with stained glass and mirrors) were quite stunning. Nothing like it had been seen before.

Although Art Nouveau was interpreted in different ways in the various countries of Europe and in the United States, certain elements were common. Floralism generally dominated the style: motifs of branches, flowers, leaves and stems proliferated, as did images of the female form.

Despite the sinuosity, most Art Nouveau interiors were quite soberly decorated, their ornamentation being generally flat and two-dimensional. They were characterized by a stress on verticals, a tendency accentuated through the division of walls using pilasters, moulding or panels of wallpaper or stencilwork. White paint was ubiquitous, although a frequently used alternative colour scheme featured grey-green relieved with salmon pink. Frieze patterns, depicting stylized natural or organic forms, were common. Furniture was no longer deep-buttoned. Fitted carpets were no longer fashionable: instead, rugs were thrown over either floorboards (customarily stained, varnished or wax-polished) or parquet flooring. The heavy draperies of the previous decades were outmoded: curtaining was simple and pelmets (cornices) flat. Stained glass, with curved leading, abounded, as did leaded glass windows with plain or coloured glass.

A turn-of-the-century Tiffany table lamp with glass shades.

An imaginative selection of decorative Art Nouveau ornaments.

A Spanish design for a comparatively simple Art Nouveau cabinet.

A stunning collection of Art Nouveau furniture and ceramics adorn this French dining-room.

FRENCH ART NOUVEAU

Also called *Le Style Moderne,* French Art Nouveau was characterized by the combination of a nostalgia for Rococo and an almost obsessive interest in vegetal forms: the result was a particularly elaborate form of decoration. Interestingly, the city of Nancy was at this time as important as Paris in terms of the new style, because of the pre-eminent École de Nancy and its many craftsmen – such as the glassworker Emile Gallé (1836–1904) – who set out to bridge the increasing gap between industry and the designer. Gallé's union of Japanese influences with a hint of Rococo and floral motifs produced a particularly distinctive style.

As in Britain, there were a number of enterprising stores, quite apart from Bing's, that sold designs by groups of artists and craftsmen: the vegetal glass of Gallé, the exquisite painted finishes of Georges de Feure (1868–1943), and the silver, exotic velvets, ceramics and wallpaper of Alphonse Mucha (1860–1939). But equally there were several designers producing integrated room schemes as well as product design, such as Mucha himself, Hector Guimard (1867–1942) and Eugène Gaillard (1862–1933). Guimard was, and indeed is, especially known for his spendid ironwork Metro station signs, many of which are still extant. Like Tiffany in the United States and Antoni Gaudí in Spain, his shapes followed the often erratic growth patterns of plants, and his mirrors and doorcases seemed to grow out of the framework of a room in a writhing, wayward fashion of their own.

CHARLES RENNIE MACKINTOSH AND THE GLASGOW SCHOOL

In Scotland Charles Rennie Mackintosh (1868–1928) and Mackay Hugh Baillie Scott (1865–1945) were busy with work that was greatly admired in Europe. Their designs were much touted by the German Hermann Muthesius in his influential three-volume *Das Englische Haus* (1904–5).

At the age of 28 Mackintosh had been commissioned by his old teacher at the Glasgow School of Art, Francis Newbury, to design a new building for the school. The result is thought by some to be one of the great masterpieces of early modern architecture. Mackintosh was fortunate, too, to have an admiring private patron, Catherine Cranston, who commissioned him and his friend George Walton (1867–1933) to design the tearooms she opened.

Mackintosh's style, which somehow managed to combine restraint with sensuality and an extraordinary sensibility to spatial relationships, had certain trademarks. These included stiff vertical lines with curvaceous infills of pink, lilac and white, almost non-existent cornices (crown moldings) forming paper-thin ledges around a room, and elongated ascetic forms which could be either human or floral. He drew inspiration from a variety of sources, particularly the Celtic and Scottish Baronial, evident in his versions of traditional inglenooks and the designs of his built-in furniture. It was altogether different from the homespun productions of the Arts and Crafts movement, although his early furniture certainly followed guidelines laid down by Morris. Mackintosh cared much more for line and decoration than for craftsmanship.

The 'feel' of the designs by Mackintosh and his colleagues in the Glasgow School was translated in diluted form into furniture and accessories, ceramics and art glass. These items were initially distributed in southern England through a large firm of cabinet-makers called Wylie and Lockhead. The company likewise sold furniture by Liberty and the Silver Studio and pieces by Ashbee to the north of the country. Other adventurous manufacturers and retailers such as Heal and Liberty started making and stocking the new lighter pieces with some success.

ABOVE The entrance hall to Hill House, Helensburgh, demonstrates typical Rennie Mackintosh finishing touches such as painted wall panels and tiny pieces of coloured glass inserted into the door.
LEFT Vertical lines and decorated panels, such as those found in Hill House, Helensburgh, became Mackintosh's hallmark.

ELSEWHERE IN EUROPE

Mackintosh's popularity burgeoned abroad. It was particularly well received in Austria, where in Vienna the Secession was created by Josef Hoffmann (1870–1955), Joseph Maria Olbrich (1867–1908) and Otto Wagner (1841–1918); these men especially prized Mackintosh's unique mixture of functionalism, austerity and elegance because they disliked the somewhat florid and languid vegetal motifs of the Belgians and French. All three were determined to break with nineteenth-century eclecticism and the

This Art Nouveau design for a bedroom by Will Bradley appeared in 1906.

conservatism hitherto somewhat prevalent in Austria.

Mackintosh was influential in Germany, too. Here Art Nouveau was called Jugendstil, after the review *Jugend* (established 1896), which was the mouthpiece for young artists and defended the floral style and its symbolism. Initially it was supported by artists such as Herman Obrist (1862–1927), who produced gnarled furniture of robust but supple form, and Otto Eckmann (1865–1902), whose arabesques bedecked furniture, wallpapers and tapestries. However, when craftsmen were called from all over Europe to work under Joseph Maria Olbrich on the decoration of the new palace at Darmstadt, the Mathildenhof, Jugendstil took on a character far removed from floralism. Instead, structure asserted itself over decoration.

In Holland, too, Art Nouveau seemed to take a sparer, almost expressionistic line, in the work of Hendrick Berlage (1856–1934) and Henry Van der Velde (1863–1957). Berlage, who designed much furniture for a studio in Amsterdam known as 'The Interior' (*Het Binnenhuis*) was particularly concerned with the influences of folk art and decorative tradition.

Van der Velde, who moved to Germany in 1899, was inspired by William Morris's ideals. He tried to eradicate rather than create ornament – an approach that gained him many pre-Bauhaus admirers.

In Italy, Art Nouveau had a great vogue, being known variously as Il Liberty (a great compliment to Liberty's store) or Lo Stile Floreale, which it certainly was. Although there were no outstanding practitioners, typical motifs appeared in and on all sorts of buildings. The Italian version was based on a hybrid of Art Nouveau styles, including those of Mackintosh, the more austere Secessionists and the highly florid French.

The strongest designer of them all, however, was the Spanish artist Antoni Gaudí (1852–1926), who worked in Barcelona and is best known for his extraordinary Sagrada Familia basilica and his apartment buildings like Casa Milá. He derived many of his motifs from local traditions, just as Mackintosh did, but in Gaudí's case they were Gothic and Moorish. His rooms have virtually no right angles, nor do they seem to follow any logic, yet they are often very beautiful and continue to amaze.

EARLY ARTS AND
CRAFTS AT
WIGHTWICK MANOR,
WEST MIDLANDS, 1878.

CEILING PAINTED
WHITE

DECORATIVE
PLASTERWORK

SIMPLE WALL
SCONCES FOR GENTLE
LIGHTING

MEDIEVAL-INSPIRED
STAINED-GLASS
WINDOWS

POLISHED WOODEN
PANELLING COVERS
THE WALLS

BENCHSEATS LINE THE
WINDOW ALCOVE

WILLIAM MORRIS
FABRICS FOR THE
UPHOLSTERY

ORIENTAL-STYLE RUGS
ON THE PARQUET
FLOOR

WORTHY MOTTOES
ABOVE THE FIREPLACE

ARTS AND CRAFTS

CREATING THE STYLE

The Arts and Crafts movement is particularly popular at the moment. In Britain it encompasses two variations: first, the style characterized by the 'crafted' work of William Morris and heavily painted medieval-inspired furnishings of the 1860s and 1870s; second, the style current between the 1880s and the beginning of the twentieth century, which has a more robust, structurally honest appearance. In the United States, the style, exemplified by the work of Gustav Stickley, consists of very austere, country-inspired furniture. There were similar craft-led movements elsewhere in Europe.

The modern popularity of the style has encouraged manufacturers to reproduce sympathetic fabrics and wallpapers. Similarly, new furniture inspired by the Arts and Crafts movement is now available – a commendable venture, since the original pieces have become so prized that now they are often more expensive than many considerably older items.

Sturdy oak furniture, typical of the Arts and Crafts period, in a renovated American barn.

HAND-PRINTED
FABRIC HANGING
FROM THE
FIRESURROUND

CARVED
MANTELSHELF
SURROUNDS WILLIAM
DE MORGAN TILES

Ceramic tiles surround the fireplace

Relief tiles and a painted overmantel create an elaborate centrepiece.

FIREPLACES

At the time – the late Victorian period – when black-leaded or painted cast-iron fireplaces were common in ordinary homes, devotees of the Arts and Crafts movement favoured wooden chimney-pieces and huge, wide hearths filled with free-standing grates and substantial andirons. These massive fireplaces dominated the architectural arrangement of rooms, and were often set in a recessed area, or inglenook, furnished with seats at either side. Hearths were generally of plain glazed bricks; above would be overhanging canopies of beaten copper. Some type of worthy motto might well be carved over the hearth. Obviously, such fireplaces would be difficult to install today. If you are lucky enough to live in an Arts and Crafts inspired house, it might be worthwhile scratching off a tiny area of paint to see if any interesting characteristics have been painted over. Slate fireplaces, sometimes with inset marble tiles, came in after 1880; by 1890 cast-iron models were also popular in many households.

Arts and Crafts influence can be detected in the 'artistic' scrolls, flowers, fruit and leaves which decorated many fire-surrounds in the late nineteenth century. Cast-iron models often had bold floral tiles inset; classic examples of these are the vivid sunflower designs by Walter Crane.

WINDOWS

Towards the end of the century pre-Georgian styles came into fashion, notably the oriel window with its shallow projecting bay and leaded panes. An 'old English cottage' look was actively sought: casement windows and leaded lights were popular. Bay windows often incorporated window-seats, the entire area forming an alcove or 'cosy corner'. Stained glass featured widely as an expression of medievalism.

DECORATIVE DETAILS

The movement's emphasis was on traditional craft skills and pre-industrial styles. Rooms were generally lower, or were visually lowered. This can be done by

Stained glass evokes a medieval atmosphere.

Panelling creates an intimate corner.

Polished wood and sombre paint in a house based on Gustav Stickley's designs.

having a deep frieze marked out by a picture-rail at the height of the door; alternatively, you could have a high dado (wainscoting). Ceilings might be half-timbered, with exposed rather than painted beams, or decorated with ornamental plasterwork reminiscent of Jacobean designs. Beams might have mottoes painted on them. Other interior finishes can be rough or glazed bricks or (less practicably!) panels of beaten copper.

FLOORS

Floorboards in Arts and Crafts houses are generally lighter than in other late Victorian homes. Oak or English woods, polished or lightly stained, were preferred. If your floorboards are suitable, and you choose to treat them this way, complete the picture using Oriental or handwoven rugs.

● Lightly stain floorboards to resemble oak and keep them well polished

TILES

William de Morgan was one of the most influential ceramicists of the movement. Tile designs to look out for include stylized flowers, Middle Eastern motifs and galleons, often executed in bright 'Persian' colours such as turquoise, green, blue, purple and coppery red. Reproductions of these designs and many others are common and originals can often be found through architectural salvage companies.

WALL COVERINGS AND FABRIC EFFECTS

Neutral colours and a period lamp create a sympathetic setting.

Handsome green panelling provides an authentic backdrop for this fine inlaid cabinet.

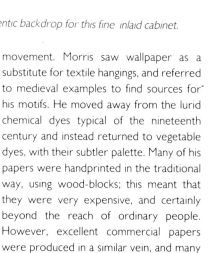

A beautifully crafted half-tester bed.

PANELLING

Wood panelling was widely adopted in the revival of the medieval style. It was available off-the-peg for the cladding of dining-rooms and halls, and usually extended to shoulder height with a flat edge. If you are lucky enough to have panelling, it should be painted dull-green or greeny-blue or stained and varnished in a dark shade to give rooms an 'antique' appearance.

WALLPAPER AND FABRIC

Paper is the standard wall covering. Contrasting in plain areas can help lighten the general effect of an Arts and Crafts interior.

The rhythmic, naturalistic wallpaper designs of William Morris are almost synonymous with the Arts and Crafts movement. Morris saw wallpaper as a substitute for textile hangings, and referred to medieval examples to find sources for his motifs. He moved away from the lurid chemical dyes typical of the nineteenth century and instead returned to vegetable dyes, with their subtler palette. Many of his papers were handprinted in the traditional way, using wood-blocks; this meant that they were very expensive, and certainly beyond the reach of ordinary people. However, excellent commercial papers were produced in a similar vein, and many Morris designs are still available today.

Walter Crane's wallpaper designs, which prefigured Art Nouveau (see page 164) in their simple stylization, were very popular in the United States. Relief papers continued to be used, especially for suggesting the effect of decorative ceiling plasterwork, although Arts and Crafts purists shunned them. Papers were also produced to co-ordinate with the designs of cretonne.

The frieze, which can be up to 1.2 m (4 ft) deep, is one of the most important elements in wall decoration. Special frieze papers were produced featuring large horizontal patterns of landscapes or stylized trees. Other frieze treatments included stencilled grass paper. Embossed plain paper would be entirely appropriate.

● If you fix a picture rail at about door height, you can either hang paper below the rail or have plain paint below and a deep frieze above

Arts and Crafts colour palette

Appliquéd and embroidered curtains provide the finishing touches.

PAINT

Artists, aesthetes and Arts and Crafts practitioners often chose colours for their ability to generate mood and atmosphere. This was a relatively new idea in interior decoration. There was a general revolt from the oppressive, gloomy late Victorian décor with its rich crimsons, gilts and dark browns. Consequently, lighter and more 'natural' schemes should be adopted to recreate an authentic atmosphere.

Aesthetic interiors can feature dull green woodwork for skirtings (baseboards), doors and chair-rails. Dados (wainscoting), too, are typically olive green. To capture a later style, paint the woodwork a creamy shade of white.

Quite sharp and unusual contrasts can enliven what is still essentially a sombre, if less oppressive, palette: deep blue and brown, black and sage green, ochre and purple, and gold and sharp green are among the combinations to use.

SOFT FURNISHINGS

The use of fabric was dramatically simplified in the Arts and Crafts interior. Furniture, fireplaces, mirrors and alcoves should be devoid of frills and flounces and window treatments should be lighter and much less fussy, fitted on plain wooden or brass poles. Heavy drapery is abandoned in favour of simple gathered curtains with plain, shaped or pleated pelmets or simply hung on plain wooden brass poles. Also, you could have little casement curtains. Suitable fabrics are silk and cretonne in popular floral patterns.

Upholstery, too, was simplified by the Arts and Crafts movement. Wooden bench- or settle-seats can be close-covered. Stamped leather, hand-weaves, printed velvets and cretonnes are desirable upholstery materials. Chintz can be used year-round rather than relegated to the bedroom or restricted to use as a summer covering. You might like to feature a chintz or a suitable fabric hanging suspended like a tapestry from the picture-rail.

● Casement curtains, perhaps in two tiers, can be fitted across a window
● Large-scale pattern fabrics with deep coloured, organic designs are the most appropriate for an Arts and Crafts interior

CRAFTSMANSHIP AND DESIGN
CREATING THE STYLE: ARTS AND CRAFTS

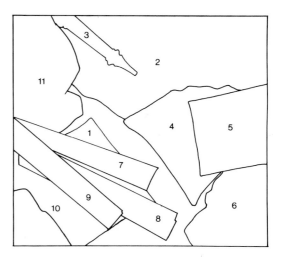

1 cotton and linen blend; 2 printed cotton; 3 Arts and Crafts chair leg; 4 antique cushion; 5 printed cotton; 6 printed cotton; 7 hand-printed wallpaper; 8 hand-printed wallpaper; 9 hand-printed wallpaper; 10 printed linen; 11 printed cotton.

A return to natural materials and colours dominated the Arts and Crafts movement. Rooms were decorated in earthy tones to set off beautifully crafted oak furniture and decorative objects in silver, pewter or brass.
Walls were often fitted with panelling which was either left plain or painted a characteristic olive green or brown. Friezes were frequently embellished with hand-painted or stencilled designs and sometimes with 'improving' mottoes. Wallpapers followed the natural theme and were decorated with foliage, animals or birds.
Fashionable upholstery was simple and close-covered, using strong linens, cottons or needlework. Curtains hung from simple poles with none of the frills and flounces of previous generations. They were often left unlined so that they could fall in soft folds, the finishing touch being provided by a plain pelmet.

FURNITURE AND FITTINGS

TYPES OF FURNITURE

As early as 1868 Charles Lock Eastlake was advocating a return to simpler furniture, honestly made and with little surface ornament. In the succeeding decades, this enthusiasm for hand-crafted work grew until, in the 1890s, new companies such as Heals and Liberty brought the results to a wider public.

William Morris's company designed furniture in the 'old English woods' of oak, elm and yew, modelled on cottage or farm-house pieces. Morris and others in the Arts and Crafts movement believed in joiner-made furniture, where no part of the construction was concealed and each item was made in its entirety by the same person. Any decoration took the form of simpli-fied, incised Gothic motifs; fittings, such as metal strap hinges, were large and obvious. This 'modified Gothic' was popular also in the United States where, about the turn of the century, Gustav Stickley had consider-able commercial success with his plain and forthright oak furniture.

A medieval-style refectory table would be ideal for the dining-room. Chairs can be simple rush-seated farmhouse designs.

This fine oak settee, heaped with plump cushions in earthy tones of gold and terracotta, is in keeping with the curtain fabric.

Simple, lantern-style hall lights of this kind enjoyed great popularity

A splendid copper light fitting with eight small electric bulbs

Four small copper lanterns make up this Arts and Crafts equivalent of a chandelier

Cupboards (perhaps with curtained shelves), cabinets and wash-stands should be, where possible, built-in rather than free-standing and of plain 'no-nonsense' construction. Wooden rather than metal bedsteads are part of the ethos.

As for other woodwork, green is the preferred colour for painted furniture, although alternatively you can opt for a natural wood finish.

DECORATIVE OBJECTS

In keeping with the general emphasis on 'honesty' and aestheticism, Arts and Crafts interiors are much less cluttered than their Victorian counterparts. The Orient, particularly Japan, is an important decorative influence, so blue-and-white porcelain, palm-leaf fans and screens should be much in evidence. At the same time, though, make sure there are a few well-selected pieces of craft pottery in the interior. Objects like vases and mirrors in materials such as pewter, silver, beaten copper and brass would be in keeping with the style.

A solitary lily in a pot provides a distinctive feature of the aesthetic interior. A potted palm would add a nice touch.

William Morris's striking acanthus leaf wallpaper with a draped bed.

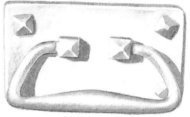

Natural finishes are emphasized in this Gustav Stickley-inspired room.

Ironwork fittings, typical of those used by followers of the craft movement

RECREATION OF AN
ART NOUVEAU
BEDROOM IN
CONNECTICUT

COLOURFUL PAINT
WASHES FOR THE
WALLS AND CEILING

PLAIN BLINDS FOR THE
WINDOW

TIFFANY-STYLE FLOOR
AND TABLE LAMPS

TALL FLOOR LAMP
FOR SUBTLE LIGHTING

ORIENTAL-INSPIRED
FURNISHING FABRICS,
COMPLETE WITH
TASSEL TRIM

SIMPLE WOODEN
FLOOR

DELICATE FRIEZE
ABOVE THE SKIRTING
BOARD

CARVED AND INLAID
BEDROOM FURNITURE

ART NOUVEAU

CREATING THE STYLE

Art Nouveau, which flowered from roughly 1892 to the early 1900s, was one of the first styles to owe virtually nothing to historical precedent. The movement derived its name from the title of the Parisian shop owned by Siegfried Bing which sold designs in the new style. This new style was particularly popular in France and Belgium. With its undulating curves and tendrils and vegetal and floriate shapes, it depended (like the Rococo) on a synthesis of exterior and interior decoration and furnishings. Of course, today, this is not such an important consideration if you want to create an Art Nouveau interior – in fact, the total look can be somewhat overpowering.

Art Nouveau ranges in style from the expressive French extremes to the more controlled compositions of Charles Rennie Mackintosh and the early work of Josef Hoffmann. Today, both Mackintosh and Hoffmann are considered precursors of the Modern Movement (see page 185). Their twentieth-century furniture classics are reproduced by the best Italian manufacturers – and are very expensive. However, their particular breed of design, along with much of Art Nouveau, can be recreated quite satisfactorily using the less costly tools of paint, wallpaper and fabric. Somewhere between the florid embellishments of French Art Nouveau and the massive rectilinearity of Hoffmann's designs was the German movement Jugendstil. This style successfully combined delicate Art Nouveau decoration with solid, more functional-looking pieces of furniture.

FURNITURE MADE FROM 'GRAINY' WOOD

Light shining through the elaborate stained-glass doors in a grand Belgian house.

165

Symmetrically styled fireplace, c 1900

Cast-iron fireplace incorporating organic motifs, c 1900

The authentic period style is accentuated by a pair of contemporary andirons.

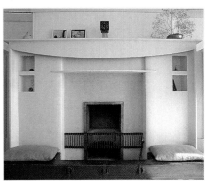

Mackintosh's inspired design.

FIREPLACES

The sinuous curves of Art Nouveau can be expressed in all types of metalwork associated with fireplaces: in the design of surrounds, coal baskets and andirons. Alternatively, at its simplest Art Nouveau influence might be expressed merely by the use of tiles with typical organic motifs inset in cast-iron surrounds.

Another version of the style was rectilinear, influenced by the work of Charles Rennie Mackintosh and the Glasgow School. Fireplaces were elongated with the emphasis on the long mantelpiece. Inglenooks, too, were common; they consisted of recesses fitted with built-in settles.

STAIRCASES

Art Nouveau was particularly prevalent in grand entrances to public buildings and the common areas of apartment blocks, spaces which tend to be dominated by stairways. Indeed, some of the most distinctive features of European Art Nouveau interiors are the flowing, organically shaped staircases created for apartment blocks and the like. Examples can be seen in interiors designed by Antoni Gaudí in Barcelona and Victor Horta in Belgium. Again, curved metal and woodwork were used to display Art Nouveau 'whiplash' motifs to advantage. Staircases were further embellished with coloured mosaic, broken ceramic, mirror and glass.

DOORS AND WINDOWS

Organic, squat or flowing shapes were a feature of European door and window openings, whereas narrow, vertically stressed shapes were more typical of the work of Mackintosh and his followers. Cheap plate glass and the development of the metal window-frame enabled curving shapes to be freely executed. Where possible, make coloured, etched and painted glass a strong feature of both doors and windows. Overt hinges, catches and handles, evidence of the influences of the Arts and Crafts movement, are other desirable characteristics.

DECORATIVE DETAILS

Ornaments should be chiefly flat and applied, rather than incorporated into the fabric, although Gaudí's compositions were plastic and modelled. Stylized floral and figurative motifs are characteristic; shapes distilled from Celtic art would emulate aspects of Mackintosh's work. Asymmetry is typical.

In the Glasgow School of Art Nouveau, attenuated verticals are very important. Pilasters, mouldings and borders can be introduced to give this emphasis to interiors. If possible, there should be panelling rising up to a deep frieze; the individual panels can be decorated with stylized flower forms.

This decorative glass overmantel creates a charming focal point.

The exotic curves are emphasized by the stylized floral border.

167

WALL COVERINGS AND FABRIC EFFECTS

Wallpaper in a bold naturalistic design forms a strong backdrop for furniture in the style of Louis Majorelle.

Silver-grey upholstery complements the highly decorated surfaces in this Rennie Mackintosh room.

WALLPAPER

The complicated organic designs of Arts and Crafts practitioners gave way to simpler, formal patterns in light colours on pale grounds. Most Art Nouveau papers display stylized flowers, foliage or seed-heads – a non-naturalistic, two-dimensional type of representation. Imitation of other materials – such as plaster, stone and wood – is scorned. The flatness of many patterns reveals a Japanese influence.

PAINT

The general lightening of room decoration, which began with the Arts and Crafts movement, continues in Art Nouveau, along with the aesthetic notion that colour can be used to provoke mood in interiors. For the first time, white became associated with a progressive spirit in design and decoration, notably with the Glasgow School, whose rooms often featured white painted panelling. Other appropriate colours you can use are lilac, mauve, salmon pink, grey green, indigo and black.

A characteristically exotic Art Nouveau flower motif.

TILES

Curved Art Nouveau designs of flowers and birds were created on tiles by forming ridges to contain areas that were then filled with transparent glazes. Similar low-relief tiles can be used to embellish fireplaces, halls, kitchens and bathrooms.

FABRIC TREATMENTS

As with wallpaper, fabric patterns should consist chiefly of stylized two-dimensional designs. Another strong preference is for embroidery: free-flowing shapes can be executed in silks or wools on coarse linen, and the results used to make wall-hangings, seat-cushions or simple window drapery.

Window treatments should not be elaborate. Shaped flat pelmets (cornices) decorated with Art Nouveau motifs are desirable and curtains should be simple.

● For an Art Nouveau effect whiplash motifs and stylized patterns can be painted flat on the surface of a wall, perhaps up a staircase or in the corner of a room

Art Nouveau colour palette

A selection of popular Art Nouveau motifs

CRAFTSMANSHIP AND DESIGN
CREATING THE STYLE: ART NOUVEAU

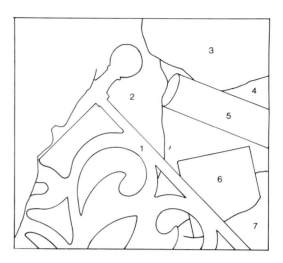

1 cast-iron railing; 2 printed cotton; 3 printed cotton; 4 hand-printed wallpaper; 5 hand-printed wallpaper; 6 Art Nouveau ceramic tile; 7 printed cotton.

An emphasis on line and form dominated the Art Nouveau, as the clutter and nick-nacks of previous generations were swept away. Walls were painted either plain white, or in colours taken from nature – rich purples, greens, ochres and browns. Much use was made of wall painting in sinuous, organic designs, mirroring the twisting lines of furniture and metalwork. Simple, formal wallpaper patterns with a flat, two-dimensional appearance proved the most popular. They usually incorporated stylized flower, foliage or seedhead motifs. Fabrics either reflected wallpaper designs or were plain, sometimes with appropriate motifs appliquéd or emboidered onto them. Windows, which were frequently adorned with stained glass or decorative lead work, were treated simply, with curtains often being abandoned altogether.

FURNITURE AND FITTINGS

Leaded windows and angular, black furniture in a room designed by Mackintosh.

TYPES OF FURNITURE

For the ordinary person, a piece of furniture in the 'New Art' style was a more accessible way of appreciating Art Nouveau than its architectural manifestations. Such commercial versions of Art Nouveau were offered by leading stores such as Liberty in London. In Paris, Samuel Bing's shop *Salon de l'Art Nouveau* promoted the work of designers working in the new style such as Georges de Feure.

The furniture designs of Mackintosh remain the most distinctive of all from the Art Nouveau period. His pieces were very exaggerated and elongated. Chairs had tall backs and pierced supports. They were often painted black or enamelled white, though sometimes they were painted surprising colours, like clear blue. Sometimes there would be incised Celtic-style decoration or opaque inserts of coloured glass. Today, reproduction of Mackintosh's

Objects add an Art Nouveau accent.

designs together with Mackintosh -inspired designs are widely available.

Working at the same time and in a similar geometric manner was the Austrian architect Josef Hoffmann, who went on to found the influential *Wiener Werkstätte*. His avant-garde designs, which look so modern today, predate the Bauhaus by 20 years.

But much of what was commercially available is less rigorously styled and less intellectually based. Beds, for example, might have curving top rails ending in floral scrolls; tables and chairs often feature spade- or heart-shaped cutouts; there are obvious hinges, catches in beaten copper, panels of stained glass, and incised mottoes decorating sideboards and cupboards. Thonet bentwood furniture likewise is in keeping with the style.

• Vases of peacock feathers give an Aesthetic look to a living room

LIGHTING

Gas remained the chief light source, although electricity was just beginning to be installed in fashionable and wealthy homes. The brief period of Art Nouveau was responsible for some magnificent and original gas and electric fittings, many making use of coloured glass. The most famous designer in this idiom was L C Tiffany of New York; his name remains associated with a particular kind of stained-glass pendant and glass table-lamp. Emile Gallé in France and William Benson in Britain worked along similar lines. Originals – though somewhat expensive – and reproductions can be purchased.

DECORATIVE OBJECTS

A great deal of domestic ware in silver, pewter and ceramic was produced in the Art Nouveau style. It should not be too hard to find appropriate pieces today. Rooms should be much less cluttered: a few well chosen pieces should take pride of place rather than be lost in a general mélange. Japanese prints, framed in deep mounts, would definitely contribute to the overall Art Nouveau impression.

A perfect setting for a stunning collection of Art Nouveau vases.

Table lamp with glass shade

Tiffany-style table lamp

Tiffany-style lampshade

A selection of Art Nouveau lighting

EDWARDIAN
FURNISHINGS IN A
LATE NINETEENTH-
CENTURY LIVING
ROOM

CENTRAL PENDANT
LIGHT FITTING WITH
SMOKED-GLASS
SHADES

WALLS PAINTED A
DIRTY GREEN

A MANTELSHELF
COVERED WITH
CONTEMPORARY
DECORATIVE OBJECTS

DRIED HONESTY
FLOWER
ARRANGEMENT

BAMBOO AND WICKER
CHAIRS AND SIDE-
TABLES

ORIENTAL-INSPIRED
RUG FOR THE FLOOR

PLUMP CUSHIONS ON
A GENEROUS SOFA

A FRINGED SHAWL
DRAPED
STRATEGICALLY

174

EDWARDIAN

CREATING THE STYLE

Three distinct styles dominated interiors at the turn of the century. They are differentiated largely on the basis of scale, but share certain telling characteristics.

In Britain, as in the United States, many large and comfortable country houses were built at this time. These were lavishly furnished, often having dining-rooms containing huge mahogany tables and sideboards, bedrooms with vast mahogany beds and needlework carpets, and smoking-rooms with Turkish and Moorish furnishings. The slightly less well off had a choice. They could opt for the matured 'Queen Anne' style, with its light paintwork, reproduction eighteenth-century furniture and fabrics and wallpaper inspired by the Arts and Crafts movement. Further down the scale, the interiors of the many small terraced houses that were built at this time could take inspiration from grander models: elements of watered-down Arts and Crafts predominated, but there were also Art Nouveau motifs that could be used on fabrics and firesurrounds.

For those who find the over-ornamentation of the Victorian upholstered style overpowering, the turn-of-the-century Edwardian style is less cluttered and consequently easier to recreate.

NEEDLEPOINT AND
EMBROIDERED
CUSHION COVERS

INDOOR POTTED
PALM TO COMPLETE
THE SCHEME

Deeply carved turn-of-the-century sideboard, completed with many porcelain ornaments.

ARCHITECTURAL ELEMENTS

Ornate cast-iron Neo-Georgian fireplace, c 1905

Cast-iron fireplace with ceramic tiles, c 1900

This white marble fireplace is adorned with traditional accessories – a brass coal scuttle and a well-polished fender

FIREPLACES

Grates were by this time relatively small and rectangular, with inclined backs and splayed sides. Around 1900, an iron or copper hood, projecting over the fire-basket, became a standard feature. Most of the mass-produced fireplaces were of cast iron and incorporated panels of decorative tiles, with smaller models for bedrooms often being cast in one piece; to emulate either the late 'Queen Anne' or the Arts and Crafts style, however, wood is the preferred material.

Classical or 'Renaissance' designs are desirable for dining-room fireplaces. In the drawing-room the styles should be lighter and more 'feminine' – typically Rococo, 'Queen Anne' or 'Adam', ornamented with urns, swags and cherubs.

An unusual corner fireplace and cupboard in a Parisian apartment.

STAIRCASES

Staircases are typically much simpler and plainer than those characteristic of the Victorian period. Balusters should ideally be plain, straight and wooden. The newel post should be wooden with a square rather than round cross-section.

WINDOWS

Sash windows are the typical form, but casements are more in keeping for a room designed to express an 'early English' flavour. 'Queen Anne' style is displayed in narrow leaded windows and in oriel bays, which could well incorporate window-seats. Stained-glass windows were still popular, a legacy of the Arts and Crafts movement, and were often used in front doors and to light stairwells.

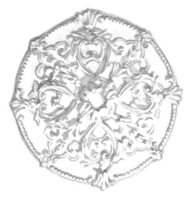

Tigbourne Court, England, designed by Sir Edward Lutyens in 1899, illustrates his interest in the light and purity of classical architecture.

Decorative plasterwork, c1900

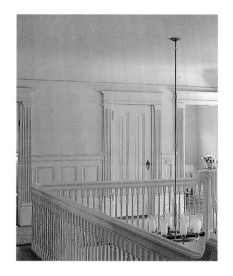

This landing shows the clean, architectural lines popular at the turn of the century.

DECORATIVE DETAILS

The fashion for antique French styles was expressed in decorative plasterwork with a Rococo appearance. 'Adam' details also abounded; they were applied to friezes, doors and chimney-pieces. In fact, 'Adam' and Regency elements of design continued to be used for decorative detail right up until World War II.

Widespread development meant that many small houses were built. As a result, decorative plasterwork – such as ceiling roses (medallions) and brackets – was correspondingly smaller in scale. Many Edwardian rooms were squarer and lower than their Victorian counterparts. Interiors could be given an 'early English' atmosphere with the use of half-timbering and Tudor- or Jacobean-style oak panelling.

FLOORS

Wood-block or parquet floors were popular at the turn of the century. If you have these types of flooring you should polish them regularly in order to build up a good sheen. Persian rugs could be used to complete the scheme.

Hand-made bricks laid in a herringbone pattern feature in some turn-of-the-century houses. This type of flooring looks effective, both left bare or 'softened' with rush matting. Red pantiles were a popular form of floor covering during this period and these are tiles that you might consider laying yourself.

In utility areas, such as a kitchen, bathroom or hall, linoleum (or vinyl) is an alternative to tiles. Hall floors can also be covered with rugs, mats or carpet-strips.

ABOVE *This room was designed by Eliel Saarinen for the President's house at Cranbrook Academy, where he became President in 1932.*
LEFT *and* FAR LEFT *Rooms in the Storer House, built by Frank Lloyd Wright in the 1920s, demonstrate his delight in space, light and interesting materials.*

THE INTERNATIONAL STYLE

The Dutch architect Gerrit Rietveld (1888–1964) admired Wright's work and was a leading member of a young group of artists, architects and designers called De Stijl ('The Style') after the avant-garde magazine of the same name. He was determined to create modern design that had no link with the past, and to achieve this end used abstract rectangular forms in primary colours. His 'Red and Blue Chair' of 1918, with its severe slab-like back and seat, was a precursor of the tactile surfaces and strong colours of Art Deco and the 1950s. But his architectural masterpiece was the Schröder House in Utrecht, finished in 1924, which – with its clean-cut surfaces devoid of mouldings and its metal-framed windows in continuous strips running up to the ceiling-level – helped formalize the new International Style.

THE FORMATION OF THE BAUHAUS

Wright's philosophies were akin to those of the German architect Walter Gropius (1883–1969), who had worked for a short time in Peter Behrens' architectural firm alongside, interestingly enough, Ludwig Mies van der Rohe and Le Corbusier. From producing a programme for using standardized parts for the mass production of small houses Gropius progressed to the reorganization of the Weimar Art School for the Grand Duke of Saxe-Weimar. This led to the founding of the Bauhaus School in 1919 and the training of a whole new generation of teachers who would in due course completely change the appearance of interiors and furniture throughout Europe. In 1925 the Bauhaus moved from Weimar to Dessau. Gropius's design for his own office in the new premises showed a general streamlining of surfaces and detail, with an emphasis on fitted furniture; the room therefore had a seemingly 'dateless' look, an effect much copied by other contemporary architects. The Bauhaus designs for chairs, light fittings and even rugs drew upon abstract art and machine imagery – for example, brightly coloured abstract-patterned rugs and austere chrome-and-leather furniture. In *The New Architecture and the Bauhaus* (1935), Gropius wrote of 'the desire for a universal style of design stemming from and expressive of an integral society and culture'.

An interior of Gerrit Rietveld's Schröder House of 1924.

MIES VAN DER ROHE AND THE MODERN MOVEMENT

Ludwig Mies van der Rohe (1886–1969), another great giant of the Modern movement, was a director of the Bauhaus from 1930. He started his career as something of a classicist; indeed, few of his buildings could withstand any alteration without a tainting of the whole, so seamlessly and beautifully were they conceived. After World War I, steel and glass became acceptable for domestic use and Mies van der Rohe, not at all in the Wright mould, used these materials and a severely restrained colour palette as an illustration of his celebrated dictum, 'Less is More.' His German Pavilion at the Barcelona International Exhibition (1929) helped establish a prototype for simple, luxurious International Style interiors. It has recently been reconstructed on its original site. Beautiful proportions and

190

Serge Chermayeff designed this Chelsea dining room in the late 1920s. His work
emphasized luxurious materials and the elimination of superfluous ornament.

sumptuous materials such as grey glass, green marble
and travertine are contrasted with steel columns
wrapped in chrome, and two reflecting pools in the
courtyard are lined with black glass. For the occasion
Mies designed some special leather chairs that have ever
since been known popularly as 'Barcelona' chairs.

With the growth of Fascism in Germany, Gropius
and other pioneers of the Modern movement, including
Marcel Breuer (1902–1981), moved temporarily to
Britain. They took the new ideas of Modernism with
them. Mies van der Rohe did the same for the United
States, to which he emigrated in 1937, being followed
in due course by Breuer and Gropius. Modernism was
now not just reserved for a small group of rarefied
architects; it became 'chic' and sophisticated, and an
emblem of the 'Free World' to a much wider audience
on both sides of the Atlantic.

Gropius's own house in Lincoln, Massachusetts, built in 1938,
demonstrates the purity of line he strove for throughout his career as
an architect and furniture designer.

191

The landing of the Villa Schwob, built by Le Corbusier in Switzerland in 1929,
demonstrates his interest in practicality and elegance of line.

ABOVE *Predominantly pale materials create a cool, harmonious interior in this house designed by Alvar Aalto in 1938.*
LEFT *A functional bathroom at the Villa Schwob.*

LE CORBUSIER

Charles Édouard Jeanneret (1887–1965), born in Switzerland, took the pseudonym of Le Corbusier. Along with the Frenchman, Auguste Perret (1874–1954), with whom he studied for a time, he was one of the great masters of the use of reinforced concrete. He settled in Paris in 1917 and made his main contribution to the International Style between the two wars, using huge strip windows, white walls, simple columns and glass bricks as fundamental ingredients of both interior and exterior composition. All these elements can be seen in his outstanding building, the Villa Savoye at Poissy-sur-Seine (1929–30).

Le Corbusier's major interest in reforming furniture and furnishings was shared by his cousin, Pierre Jeanneret (1896–1967), and Charlotte Perriand (b. 1903). Their combined design for furnishing a *unité d'habitation* (living unit), exhibited at the Salon d'Automne des Artistes-Décorateurs in Paris in 1929, though scorned by many, was a conscious and uncompromising effort to make people come to terms with 'modern' living and the advent of new technology – to create 'a machine for living' that matched the age, with built-in furniture, laminated surfaces, concealed lighting and chromium-plated steel-tube furniture. In fact, until very recently, few architects designing a 'modern' home would consider doing an interior without incorporating some of the modern-furniture classics based on the designs of Le Corbusier, Mies van der Rohe and Breuer.

ART DECO

A design taken from Interieurs
Français *of 1925.*

Modernism, however, was not the only major design movement of the early twentieth century. What was in effect its antithesis was Art Deco, so-called after the Exposition des Arts Décoratifs in Paris (1925), but actually sparked off much earlier, in 1909, by the arrival in Paris of Diaghilev's *Ballets Russes*. Leon Bakst's brightly coloured, sensuous stage sets and flamboyant costumes had an immediate effect on fashion. Leading couturiers like Paul Poiret produced harem pants, gold turbans and other clothing considerably more relaxed than that which had gone before. *La Belle Époque* gave way to slim skirts and gold lamé. But this freer, looser, exotic clothing needed exotic backgrounds to match. *Le Goût Ritz*, a kind of diluted Louis XVI style with elements from the *Directoire* and *Empire*, had hitherto been the most fashionable style of the first decade of the century. (Indeed, it remains so for many, who feel that the late – eighteenth-century French interior, with its classically inspired details and simple mouldings, can hardly be improved upon, just as the label 'Georgian' conveys the image of safe elegance to the British.) After World War I, there was an urgent need for a new sort of

look, a craving for the luxury abandoned so abruptly in 1914, and this was satisfied by Art Deco.

Art Deco (or Jazz Moderne, as it came to be called as the Jazz Age progressed) combined elements of Neoclassicism, the Orientalism and Exoticism of the *Ballets Russes*, the excitement caused by the popularity in Paris of the singer and dancer Josephine Baker, the influence of the recent archaeological discoveries in Egypt, the new dances – the Tango and the Charleston – and, through the Cubist and Fauvist painters of the period, primitive art and various African influences (Africa at that time was popular because of the newly fashionable safari trips). All these influences produced the movement's brilliant colours, the exotic finishes (the willowy bronze girls with their greyhounds, for example), the geometry, the ivories, the animal skins, the stylized sun-rays and birds, and the pyramid shapes and mouldings for radios and other ornaments. There was even a resurgence in the popularity of sphinxes.

Art Deco did not share the cohesiveness displayed by Art Nouveau and Bauhaus-inspired interiors. Instead, it was more the result of a grouping of individual elements – furniture, textiles, ornaments, ceramics and glass – against fairly simple backgrounds with classical details such as fluted columns, festoons, stylized baskets of fruit and inset plaster-relief patterns on classical or allegorical themes. Because of the advent of advanced machine technology, in particular the mass-production of motor cars, the emphasis was on speed and power, sometimes emphasized by plaster waves and muscular human figures in bronze.

Leading designers of the style in Paris included Jacques-Émile Ruhlmann (1879–1933), whose beautifully made furniture was often inlaid with exotica (lizard skin, tortoiseshell, lapiz and ivory), André Groult (1884–1967), whose decorating skills were much sought after, Jean Dunand (1877–1942), who worked in lacquer and metal, and the British designer Eileen Gray (1878–1977), who had settled in Paris. Wrought iron and bronze were often crucial to Art Deco interiors; Edgar Brandt (1880–1960) was a master of these. Armand-Albert Rateau (1882–1938), another successful designer, created a spectacular domed bath-

ABOVE Art Deco on a comfortable scale.
TOP Sensual statues atop columns.
LEFT This elegant Art Deco dining room
is furnished with a Ruhlmann cabinet.

room with a sunbeam bath carved out of a single block of white marble; it was surrounded by gold lacquered walls engraved with a herd of different animals and detailed vegetation.

Jean-Michel Frank, now a cult figure, was among the most important of the designers active towards the end of the 1920s. His pale, natural silk, parchment or undyed-leather walls, concealed lighting, contrasting textures and simply shaped but luxuriously finished furniture became enormously popular in the United States (as, indeed, did Art Deco in general). The New York of the 1920s, prior to the great stock-market crash, had all the verve of the New World, the emphasis being on opulence as much as on functionalism. Gold-plating and engraved glass, cream and gold tiles, elaborate metalwork and friezes and contrasting woods were all ingredients of work by Ralph Walter, John Wellborn Root (1850–1891) and other Jazz Age designers of the time, including the redoubtable interior decorator Elsie de Wolfe (1865–1950). In Britain Art Deco was received with slightly more restraint – Syrie Maugham, another interior decorator and wife of the novelist Somerset Maugham, was noted for her pickled and waxed white-on-white interiors.

THE PASSION FOR REVIVAL

In addition to Modernism and Art Deco, there was a further important movement in the 1920s and 1930s, this one based on a nostalgia for times past. People started to put tenderness and care into restoring old houses. Revivals included the neo-Georgian and 'Tudorbethan' in Britain and neo-Colonialism in the United States. An enormous amount of time and money was put into 'sensitive' restoration and appropriate decoration. Perhaps as an expression of genuine distaste for the razzamatazz of Art Deco or the coldness of Modernism, there developed an appreciation of 'pleasing decay', the deliberate searching after old fabrics, textiles, designs, tapestries and rugs – and, *de rigueur*, worn furniture with its gentle patina. This loose movement used an educated eye for scale and colour to create a synthesis of different styles from the past. The trend was interrupted by World War II, and only in the last few years has it reappeared as a popular decorative style in Europe and the United States.

A collection of trompe-l'oeil *painting, needlepoint and ceramics combine to create a colourful, harmonious room at Charleston, Sussex.*

These charming 1920s illustrations show fashionable inter-war styles.

The dining room ABOVE CENTRE *cultivates a cosy Elizabethan effect, while*

the bedroom ABOVE RIGHT *displays a variation on the Queen Anne revival style.*

Neo-Rococo furniture is favoured for this bathroom. This predominantly pink and green colour scheme enjoyed great popularity in the 1920s.

BUCK HOUSE, LOS
ANGELES, DESIGNED
BY RUDOLPH
SCHINDLER IN 1934

VERTICAL WINDOWS
AROUND THE TOP OF
THE ROOM

MODERN SCULPTURE
SET OFF AGAINST
WHITE WALLS

SMOOTH PLASTERED
WALLS PAINTED
WHITE

NO DECORATIVE
PLASTERWORK

DRAWERS FITTED
INTO THE WALL

LARGE PLATE-GLASS
WINDOWS AT
GROUND LEVEL

EXPOSED ROMAN
BRICKWORK AROUND
THE HEARTH

GLASS-TOPPED
COFFEE-TABLE WITH
CHROME BASE

WHITE VENETIAN
BLINDS TO SCREEN
THE LIGHT

MODERNISM

CREATING THE STYLE

Creating an authentic Modernist interior is not easy, primarily because there is no such thing as a single style called Modernism. The term was used to describe the output of a group of quite diverse architects who worked in the 1920s and 1930s. However, their themes did share certain characteristics which can be used to create, at the very least, a good sympathetic style. Glass bricks, white-painted or untreated concrete walls, plate-glass horizontal windows and ramps – these are all entirely suitable ingredients.

Above all, the style relies on little or no decorative detailing. Although a 'hard' geometric style which concedes little to the comfort of the eyes, Modernism has many attractive qualities, not least of which is its deliberate heightening of natural light.

Restoring or recreating an interior in this style can be relatively inexpensive as the main components – white walls, plain blinds for the window, simple light fittings and so on – require very little outlay.

The black leather and chrome 'Grand Confort' chair, designed by the architect, Le Corbusier, in the 1930s.

WALL-TO-WALL
FITTED CARPET IN A
PLAIN COLOUR

A BARCELONA CHAIR,
DESIGNED BY MIES
VAN DER ROHE IN 1929

199

ARCHITECTURAL ELEMENTS

This Swiss villa, designed in the 1930s, demonstrates Le Corbusier's mastery at creating an environment which is both calm and luxurious.

INTERIOR ARCHITECTURE

The designers and architects of the Modern movement insisted on a distinction between interior *architecture* and *decoration*, a distinction which arose out of the way interiors were conceived as integral expressions of the structure and function of a building. Modernist interiors do away with all types of applied decoration, concentrating on pure geometry and form. Walls should therefore be unbroken by mouldings or architraves; skirtings (baseboards) may be reduced to the narrowest margin bordering the floor. The only interruptions in the smooth planar surface of the wall might be curved segments, contrasting materials such as glass brick, wood panelling and occasionally exposed stone or brick. The effect can in many cases be exaggerated through the use of the open-plan disposition of space.

FIREPLACES

The hearth still persists as a focal point despite the general lack of the traditional domestic reference points. However, the decorative fire-surround can be abandoned in favour of a simple rectangular opening for solid-fuel fires. Alternatively, in place of a hearth there could be a built-in wall-mounted gas or electric fire. Low-level built-in cabinets and bookcases might extend to either side. Exposed radiators and heating grills could also feature.

● Although Modernist fireplaces should be simple rectangular openings, you can relieve the severity by use of a frame of white ceramic tiles or a plain slate mantelshelf
● 'Traditional' style radiators can be found at architectural salvage companies, but you can rarely find ones that match; luckily, modern versions have recently become available in a range of strong colours as well as in the more traditional white

STAIRCASES

Materials included concrete, metal tubing and tensioned wire. Deliberately functional and non-decorative, Modernist staircases nevertheless achieve a sculptural beauty.

• Stairs can be left uncovered – wooden treads will have to be treated with a strong polyurethane varnish – or can be 'softened' with a strip of plain-coloured carpet

DOORS AND WINDOWS

Glass is one of the key materials of Modernism, and many writers of the time referred to the period as the 'age of glass'. Improvements in the manufacture of glass made larger glazed expanses possible, and metal-framed windows began to be used.

Picture windows, long strip windows, casements and portholes are some of the Modernist shapes. Elevations often have a faintly nautical air.

Glazed or partly glazed doors are also suitable. Internal doors should be flush, not panelled; their plain functional look is in keeping with the aesthetic.

• Door and window furniture should be very simple; there are few 'true' Modernist designs for these, but some of the more recent High-tech designs can be used

FLOORS

Flooring should be a neat, seamless background, linking spaces together. Appropriate materials include linoleum, hardwood strip flooring, and hard-wearing quarry or ceramic tiles.

• Wooden strip flooring in a pale colour can provide a good neutral background for colourful rugs in abstract designs

ABOVE An Alvar Aalto 1930s interior. TOP Frank Lloyd Wright's stark Storer House, Pasadena.

WALL COVERINGS AND FABRIC EFFECTS

PAINT

According to Le Corbusier, writing in the 1920s, the only acceptable treatment for walls is for them to be painted white. This also proved popular with fashionable contemporary decorators such as Syrie Maugham whose all-white Chelsea living room (1929) became so influential partly because it succeeded in combining the Modernist love of pure white and luxurious materials with traditional furnishings and comfort. Plain white plastered walls are the hallmark of Modernist interiors.

However, some colour can appear on walls. Contrasting shades can be used to articulate different areas within a large space. Exploiting the concept whereby strong warm tones ('advancing colours') bring out a feature or pale cool shades ('retreating colours') make an area recede is also appropriate.

Skirting boards (baseboards), if present, are usually painted to blend in with the wall. Occasionally, however, they can be painted in a dark colour or black.

- If you are attempting to create a Modernist scheme in a room dating from an earlier period, do not be tempted to pull out existing features, because you may regret it later; for example, decorative plasterwork, such as cornices and ceiling roses, can be painted white to 'disappear' into the scheme

OTHER MATERIALS

Aside from plain rendering, walls may be covered in a range of other finishes to provide a textural interest or to express a link with the natural world, as in the architecture of Frank Lloyd Wright. Plain unpainted panelling is a good alternative to white walls. Sycamore, oak, birch and cherry are frequently used woods; detailing may be nautical in flavour.

Dark mirror glass, with obvious fixings, is another wall treatment. Wallpaper should in general be shunned, although natural fibre papers with obvious textures or grain and neutral colour can be used. These will provide a good backdrop for Modernist furniture.

- Mirrored walls are effective at enhancing natural light: you can use either large panels of mirror, to create a purer effect, or mirror tiles (available in a variety of sizes)

FABRIC TREATMENTS

The use of fabric is severely curtailed in the Modernist interior, especially compared to the highly dressed and draped rooms typical forty years earlier. Curtains, if present, should be extremely simple affairs, generally hung up from a plain track or pole and lacking any further trimming or embellishment. Roman blinds are suitably simple for a Modernist scheme. Geometric designs – spots and stripes in particular – or strong solid colours are advised, as are 'natural' weaves in neutral shades. You can opt for woollen wall hangings, like the ones the Bauhaus workshop produced.

Upholstery, too, should be restrained and controlled, with close coverings being the rule. Leather and hide can replace fabric.

- Natural fabrics in white or cream – for example, canvas – are the most suitable

ABOVE A sophisticated, metropolitan look is created by an imaginative use of black and white.
RIGHT This dining room, designed by Alvar Aalto in the 1930s, demonstrates a combination of spaciousness and practicality.

*Simple Roman blinds, flanking one of a pair of tall mirrors, help create an
overwhelming sense of airy grandeur.*

FURNITURE AND FITTINGS

Selection of 1930s-style light fittings

Glass and chrome ceiling light

Chrome wall light

Chrome standard lamp

ROOM ARRANGEMENT

The way rooms are organized and arranged should reflect the Modernist concepts of space design, with open-plan and multi-purpose areas. In any case with increasing pressure on space, having a series of separate rooms for different activities is today often no longer a practical proposition.

In Modernist interiors a large proportion of furniture is built in. Cupboards, bookcases, kitchen cabinets, sideboards and wardrobes can be fixed in position or fully integrated as closets. Tables and chairs are arranged according to the needs they serve – for example, around a rug for a conversation area. The same table in a modular design can be used for both studying and dining, with chairs being pulled up as required. In general, rooms should appear underfurnished, with a distinct lack of clutter.

TYPES OF FURNITURE

This period saw a revolution in furniture design, with a conscious abandonment of traditional materials, techniques and decoration in favour of a new machine-age aesthetic. Tubular steel, bent and laminated wood, glass and man-made products are favoured materials; among the methods of construction and design are many borrowed from industry and engineering, notably the use of the cantilever principle.

A number of the famous architectural names associated with the Modern movement also designed furniture. Pieces range from the bold but impractical statement of Rietveld's 'Red and Blue Chair' (1918) to Alvar Aalto's adaptable and ubiquitous stacking stools. Le Corbusier's designs include his *Le grand confort* chair (1928) and his well known leather- or hide-covered *chaise-longue*; Mies van der Rohe's 'Barcelona' chair and Breuer's 'Wassily' (1925) are other modern classics. Many are still manufactured under licence, although at the time they were largely rejected for domestic use.

LIGHTING

Modernism coincided with universal domestic electric lighting. The new designs for fittings were functional, non-decorative and inspired by industrial methods and materials. Modern classics such as the anglepoise first made an appearance at this time. Fixed central ceiling lights are the norm, but track light-

Le Corbusier and Charlotte Perriand's recliner of chrome and skin – the epitome of modern style.

ing is acceptable, early forms of this having appeared during the 1920s and 1930s. The United States was in the vanguard of modern light-fitting design; materials included Bakelite, Lucite, Formica, steel and chrome.

OBJECTS

'Decorative' objects are largely superfluous for Modernist interiors. However, selected craft pieces and examples of tribal or modern art can be displayed sparsely, and cacti are also suitable. During this period, nearly every household gadget and object, from ashtrays to cutlery, was tackled by designers. 'Streamlining', a concept borrowed from the aeronautical industry, was applied to the design of new appliances of all sorts – refrigerators, toasters, telephones, radios, electric fires, cookers and countless others. Some of these can be picked up in antique shops; as always, have them properly checked out before you try to use them. Reproductions are also widely available.

Carpeting can be ribbed or cord in natural or neutral shades. Oriental matting, echoing Japanese *tatami* mats is a popular option.

By contrast, rugs are much more exuberant and colourful. Influenced by modern-art trends such as Constructivism, Abstraction and Cubism, designers of the period such as Eileen Gray, Robert Mallet-Stevens, Marion Dorn and Sonia Delaunay created vivid contemporary compositions, many of which are still reproduced today. Textural handmade traditional rugs, such as kelims and Scandinavian flatweaves, are also in keeping.

KITCHEN AND BATHROOM FITTINGS

Both of these rooms should feature built-in fittings. In the kitchen you can have space-saving units, with pull-out tops that form work surfaces. At the time new gas and electric cookers replaced the old kitchen ranges. The emphasis was largely on hygiene and labour-saving design.

Bathrooms, too, were the focus of considerable design attention; the public accepted a modern look in the bathroom because here there was little traditional precedent. Surfaces should be tiled and fittings built-in.

ABOVE and TOP This Los Angeles bathroom and a kitchen designed by Alvar Aalto demonstrate that functional can also be sophisticated.

205

SIMPLE WINDOW
TREATMENTS IN PLAIN
FABRICS

MIRRORS WITHOUT
FRAMES, CUT IN
GEOMETRIC SHAPES

SHINY CHROME
FITTINGS AND
FIXTURES SUCH AS
UPLIGHTS

SOLID COLOUR FOR
THE WALLS, PERHAPS
WITH A DECORATIVE
BORDER

'STEPPED' SIDEBOARDS
AND PICTURE FRAMES

SOFA AND CHAIRS
ARRANGED IN A
CONVERSATIONAL
GROUP AROUND A
CENTRAL COFFEE
TABLE

STREAMLINED
FURNITURE TO
REFLECT THE AGE

SMOOTH POLISHED
PARQUET FLOOR LAID
IN A HERRINGBONE
PATTERN

ART DECO FIGURINES
FOR DECORATIVE
DISPLAY

APPROPRIATE
ACCESSORIES SUCH
AS BOXES AND
CIGARETTE TRAYS

ART DECO

CREATING THE STYLE

Art Deco shared some of the geometric shapes and lines of Modernism. Where it differed substantially was in its use of bright colours, such as orange and red, and in its stylised figurative decoration. Sources of inspiration included recent art movements, such as Cubism and Fauvism, as well as African tribal and central-American Aztec motifs. Well-known Art Deco designers included Paul Iribe, Pierre Legrain, Jacques-Émile Ruhlmann and Paul Poiret (the noted couturier). These designers used not only mass-produced materials such as glass and chrome, but also more exotic materials such as ivory and snakeskin. Among wealthy clients, no expense was spared in the quest to create ever-more luxurious furniture and furnishings with which to decorate their homes.

A more severe, less ornamental form of Art Deco is sometimes called Art Moderne and, arguably, can be seen as a commercial, toned-down version of Modernism. It has none of the figurative decoration of Art Deco, although, in the United States in particular, it included the 'streamlining' tendencies.

Both Art Deco and Art Moderne styles were used on a large scale for inexpensive mass-produced furniture throughout Europe and the United States. Luckily, this means that many pieces are still available today from second-hand stores. Similarly, decorative objects such as statuettes, vases and clocks – which are such important elements of the style – are widely available.

The wireless with its sunburst pattern and the Anglepoise lamp are typical of 1930s interiors.

SQUARE, ANGULAR
FURNITURE
UPHOLSTERED IN
TEXTURED FABRICS

207

ARCHITECTURAL ELEMENTS

FIREPLACES

Up until World War II coal and wood were still the main form of heating and so open fireplaces are an important aspect of the Art Deco interior. Popular mass-produced Art Deco designs feature the stepped-ziggurat profile. Surrounds were often tiled all over in buff, pale green or dusty pink. At the other end of the scale, the luxury version of Art Deco has glittering fireplaces faced in mirror mosaic or with mirrored chimney-breasts. Electric fires were at the time a common supplementary source of heating and the designs could be highly whimsical such as those made in the shape of yachts. These fires can today be purchased from antique shops, although obviously you should have them fully checked out before using them.

• Use dried flowers such as honesty to fill an empty fireplace

This sophisticated hallway makes pronounced use of vertical lines, the effect greatly enhanced by a wall of mirror.

Authentic Art Deco motifs

A spacious effect is created by the addition of a mirrored wall.

This room manages to combine comfort with Art Deco elegance.

DECORATIVE DETAILS

Art Deco encompasses at least two distinctive strands, the early high-quality manifestations of the style, which occurred largely in France, and the later mass-produced version, which was widely popular and much less coherent. The roots of the high-style version can be traced back to the *Empire* style (see page 74), coloured by Chinese and African influences. The popular version is characterized by interpretations of Cubism, Aztec and Egyptian motifs such as the pyramid or ziggurat shapes, and stylized rising suns and graphic lightning flashes.

FLOORS

Linoleum was produced in bright, abstract designs; this material is a good floor covering for the hall, kitchen and bathroom of most homes and would give an authentic period feel. Strip wooden flooring is also appropriate for an Art Deco interior, in particular for a living room or a dining room. It provides a highly suitable surface for displaying brightly coloured rugs.

● A black-and-white chequerboard floor helps to create a strong geometric look in a kitchen or a bathroom and can be created simply with vinyl tiles.

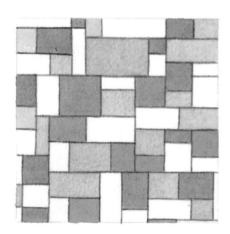

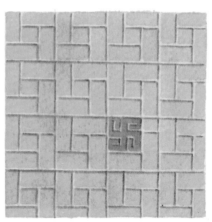

During the 1930s, linoleum was created in a variety of geometric designs

WALL COVERINGS AND FABRIC EFFECTS

Art Deco colour palette

A distinctive uplight draws attention to striking wall stencils of stylized Art Deco motifs.

WALLPAPER

Wallpaper moved gradually down-market during the 1920s and 1930s; it was generally considered not to be in the best of taste. The cult of the plain wall was so pervasive that paper manufacturers were forced to counter falling sales by introducing embossed papers, flecked with tiny nondescript patterns. Some popular mass-produced papers were less inconspicuous. Designs to choose from include chevrons, stylized leaves, flowers and fruit, Futurist motifs and 'Cubist' derivations. Appliquéd cut-outs and borders are also in keeping. Borders can run below the ceiling or picture-rail 'Growths' – cut-outs of stylized flowers and foliage – were applied around the perimeter of the room or along the length of a stairway to make it look as if they were 'growing' from the skirting-board.

PAINT

In the early 1920s Sergei Diaghilev's *Ballets Russes* had an enormous impact on fashion and decoration. The strong exotic colours of the sets and costumes – purple, jade green and orange – were adopted by the avante-gardists and the Bohemians, eager to forget the privations of World War I. These vivid colours can be set off with black or gold.

However, to recreate a late-1920s interior you should use more muted colours. Sage green, cream, stone, *eau-de-Nil* (pale greyish green), grey blue and primrose yellow are all suitable wall colours as is pure white. One sophisticated Art Deco combination is grey, black and green; however, orange with brown and cream with green were more commonplace at the time.

Plain painted walls are appropriate for sophisticated interiors; subtle shades of distemper which, when dry, gives a soft chalky finish, are entirely suitable. Kitchens and bathrooms should be decorated in an oil-based paint for best results.

FABRIC TREATMENTS

As in Modernism (see page 186), rugs are an important expression of the style. Rugs in brilliant Fauve colours, and Axminster and Brussels carpet-squares might feature repeated 'Cubist' designs and jazz motifs.

Co-ordination is an important element in a '1930s' room, with fabric, wallpaper and linoleum all in the same designs and colours. All-over abstract or geometric designs can be used as well. Typical colours include marine blue, dull green and pinkish brown.

This simply tiled cubicle creates a perfect setting for 1930s shower fittings.

ABOVE Gracious Art Deco motif.
TOP A refined corner in perfect period style.

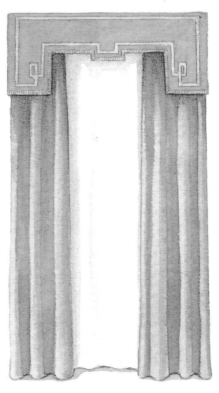

Window treatments should be fairly simple, although curtain headings may be hidden by shaped flat or pleated pelmets. Tassels are an appropriate trimming.

Cushions are a positive element in living-rooms, particularly floor cushions covered in velvet or brocade matched with shawls draped over divans, to create part of the 1920s 'Bohemian' look. Furniture can be close-covered to reveal streamlined shapes, but loose covers are also appropriate.

ABOVE and LEFT Softly gathered curtains finished with a simple pelmet were favoured in Art Deco schemes
FAR LEFT Stylized motifs were often used in Art Deco textile designs.

211

MODERN MOVEMENTS
CREATING THE STYLE: ART DECO

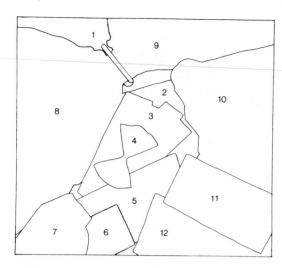

*I stainless steel: 2 textured cotton blend: 3 textured printed
cotton: 4 woven upholstery fabric: 5 printed cotton. 6 patterned
wallpaper: 7 textured cotton blend: 8 leopard-spot velour:
9 chrome handle: 10 printed silk: 11 textured cotton:
12 textured cotton blend.*

*Art Deco interiors achieved their often theatrical effect through
the use of contrast: Hard, highly polished wood, lacquer and steel
were contrasted with filmy silks, satin and real or fake leather and
furs. Interiors with little architectural detail were set off by
dramatic curtains with a heavy sheen or bold pattern.
Plain colours were popular for both walls and fabrics; but when
pattern was used it was usually in the form of a geometric design
or stylish black, white and grey we associate Art Deco was
supplemented with orange, purple, red, pink, yellow and green,
to create a sophisticated and often decadent effect.*

FURNITURE AND FITTINGS

TYPES OF FURNITURE

New types of furniture introduced during the early decades of the twentieth century included the coffee-table and the cocktail cabinet. At the popular level, the design changes were merely a matter of giving traditional furniture types Art Deco styling, using a stepped profile, smooth veneered wood and a solid rounded form. Chairs and sofas are typically low and curved, while tables have fairly massive central pillars. Glass panels and contrasting wood inlays are used for decorative flourishes.

The best Art Deco furniture was produced in France by designers such as Jacques-Emile Ruhlmann, Jean Dunand and Armand Rateau. These pieces are exquisite and luxurious, featuring the use of leather, exotic woods, mother-of-pearl and shagreen inlay and often using animal motifs, Chinese-style lacquerwork and African patterning.

DECORATIVE OBJECTS

Art Deco had a great impact on a whole range of decorative and household objects, particularly glass and ceramics. Clarice Cliff (1899 – 1972) and Susie Cooper (b. 1902) are among the best known ceramicists from the period. The name of the French designer René Lalique (1860 – 1945) is almost synonymous with fine artefacts in glass.

Ashtrays were on display for the first time, reflecting the new social acceptability of the smoking habit: pedestal designs were typical; statuettes of women in sensuous poses are also in order.

Mirrors are the perfect medium for Art Deco style. These can be hung in panels of contrasting colours and shapes that are stepped, rounded, fan or cutout. Flower arrangements should veer to the exotic: bonsai, cacti, lilies and bare branches represent the height of elegance and style.

LIGHTING

Art Deco table-and floor-lights, wall-fittings and chandeliers are available in a range of different designs. Original, high-quality work by French designers such as Lalique, Daum Frères and Ruhlmann tends to display an interest in the varying opacity of glass. Ruhlmann and Pierre Chareau (1883 – 1950) designed lights in alabaster; however, more common are shades made of frosted or opal glass coloured in pink, cream or green.

Popular Art Deco lighting designs are geometric, naturalistic or stylized crescents, sunbursts and zigzags. Chrome table-lamps and wall-mounted fan or shell light-fittings are perhaps the most common designs and can still be found in antique shops.

● During the 1930s Anglepoise or similar lamps were often fitted to the wall; you may prefer to use a desk-top Anglepoise lamp

A selection of Art Deco lighting

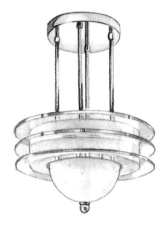

Sophisticated ceiling light

Fan-shaped wall light

Distinctive ceiling light

Great attention was paid to lighting and decorative objects in Art Deco interiors. The latter often took the form of animals associated with speed and grace, such as antelopes, horses and panthers.

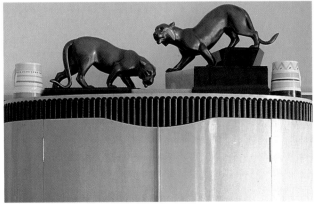

GLOSSARY

acanthus leaves The thick, scalloped leaves of *Acanthus spinosus*, used since classical times in stylized form on the tops of columns and architectural mouldings, or on furniture.

Adirondack furniture Rustic furniture produced in the mid-1800s in North America, made from roughly hewn and bent branches and logs.

Anaglypta An extremely heavily embossed wallpaper, used on walls and ceilings.

anthemion Decorative motif of Greek origin, the radiating pattern of which resembles the honeysuckle flower and leaves.

arabesque Literally 'Arabian', this refers to a Moorish pattern of interlaced branches, leaves, flowers and scrollwork. It appeared on 16th and 17th-century Spanish and Portuguese furniture before becoming popular elsewhere in Europe.

architrave This term derives from the lowest of the three parts of the **entablature** in Greek architecture. It can also refer to a decorative band surrounding a door, window-frame or mirror.

arrowback chair An American form of **Windsor chair** popular after about 1830, in which the spindles flare outward.

aumbry A cupboard with a door, used to store food.

Axminster A type of knotted pile carpet produced at Axminster in England in the late 18th and early 19th centuries. They were later made as cut-pile carpets. The designs were frequently inspired by Oriental as well as European patterns.

baluster A vertical post, a series of which forms a **balustrade.**

balustrade A series of **balusters** with a rail along the top, forming a low wall or barrier, usually made of stone or wood.

bambooing A painting technique used to make wood look like bamboo. It was highly fashionable from the mid-18th to the late 19th centuries.

baseboard See **skirting.**

beading A decorative strip of moulding frequently applied to furniture, though also found on silver, glassware and pottery as an ornamental edging.

Berlin woolwork Brightly coloured *gros-point* needlework using canvases, patterns and yarn distributed by Berlin manufacturers. It was popular during the mid-19th century.

bobbin twist A design given to turned chair stretchers, backs and legs from the 17th century onwards, which looks like a row of bobbins.

boiserie Carved wooden panelling. In Rococo and neo-Rococo interiors these would be gilded and have a white background.

Boston rocker An American rocking chair produced from the early 19th century and related to the **Windsor chair.** It had a scrolled seat and was usually decorated with stencilled patterns in bright colours.

boullework A form of **marquetry,** usually with tortoiseshell and brass. This technique, which originated in 10th-century Italy, was improved 8 centuries later by André-Charles Boulle in France. It was popular from the late 17th to the 19th centuries, when the effect was reproduced by machine.

Brussels carpet A general term for hard-wearing carpets woven with heavy wool and linen. The designs were French and they were produced from the 16th century onwards.

'C' and 'S' scrolls Motifs which imitate 'C' and 'S' shapes characteristic of the Rococo style. Found on chairs, bureaux, mirrors and picture frames.

cabriole leg A chair or table leg shaped to imitate a stylized form of animal's hind leg. It typically took the form of an elongated 'S'. The style originated in the Far East and became popular in Europe during the 17th and 18th centuries.

caryatid Female figure derived from Greek architecture which is used as a decorative support. Particularly fashionable during the Renaissance, Rococo and Neoclassical periods.

casement A type of window having, typically, one fixed pane, a small top pane that can be opened and one large pane that can be opened (usually hinged at the side).

case pieces The opposite of seat furniture, these are pieces used for storage, such as bookcases, cabinets and *chiffoniers.*

cassone Italian marriage chests, usually elaborately carved, gilt, inlaid or painted.

ceiling rose (medallion) A roughly circular ceiling decoration, usually placed centrally on the ceiling. The rose is usually of plaster and in many cases a lighting fixture may be suspended from it.

chamfered A faceted edge, often on furniture legs which are turned outwards, and produced by bevelling off an angle.

chiffonier A chest of drawers with a cupboard and doors, which also functions as a sideboard. It often has shelves and a mirror above it.

chinoiserie Refers to European designs fashionable from the late 17th century, which drew heavily on Far Eastern motifs. Fretwork, pagodas, birds, landscapes and rivers were common decorative devices.

claw-and-ball foot A furniture leg ending in the shape of a claw holding a ball. In Oriental furniture the claws are talons or a dragon's claw, whereas in European and American pieces they usually form an eagle's claw.

commode A low chest of drawers which originated in mid-17th century France and became widely popular in the 18th century. Although it was designed for the drawing-room, during the 19th century the term was also applied to a bedroom cupboard.

console A form of side-table supported by wall-brackets and two front legs.

cornice (crown molding) The part of the decoration on a wall joining the wall and the ceiling. It also refers to the horizontal moulding that projects from the top of some **case pieces.**

coved ceiling This is created when the arched junction between wall and ceiling forms a large concave, or coved, area.

crown molding see **cornice**

dado The lower part of an interior wall, between skirting and chair rail.

day-bed A couch with a single head usually in the shape of a chair back, sometimes with arms. These pieces were first made in the 17th century.

diaper motif A trellis design of squares or rectangles, sometimes containing carved motifs.

distemper A type of paint made by mixing glue and water with size, whiting etc.

GLOSSARY

divan An upholstered bench seat, of Oriental origin, popular in the Victorian era as part of a Turkish or Eastern theme.

dovetail joint A right-angled joint with interlocking dovetail- or fan- shaped tenons. From the 18th century onwards these were often concealed by a flat overlapping piece of wood for furniture of high quality.

dragged finish A paint finish created by dragging a dry brush over a wet glaze, usually vertically. In appearance, it is reminiscent of fabric covering.

drum-top table A round table on a tripod stand, with a deep top that often holds drawers. Usually of Neoclassical origin.

ebonized wood Also called *bois noirci*, this is wood stained black to imitate ebony. It was used frequently on Victorian Oriental style cabinets, chairs and tables.

egg-and-dart moulding Also known as egg-and-tongue, this is a common classical motif used on architecture and furniture. It consists of repeated oval shapes alternated with dart shapes.

eggshell (semi-gloss) paint An oil-based paint with a mid-sheen finish – halfway between matt and gloss.

emulsion (latex) paint Water-based paint used principally to cover walls and ceilings.

entablature The whole section above the capitals of a column, i.e. the **architrave, frieze** and **cornice.** The term is applied to the equivalent part of a cabinet or cupboard.

étagère A set of shelves, free-standing or attached to the wall, on which objects are displayed. Sometimes it has glazed doors.

faux finishes See **graining, marbling.**

Favrile glass The tradename given by Tiffany to his blown **iridescent glass,** usually vases, in the late 19th century.

festoon Also known as a swag, this design appears on Renaissance and Neoclassical furniture, and imitates a loop of drapery or a garland of fruit and flowers.

filigree A lacy effect produced from curled and twisted metal wire, or openwork in porcelain.

fluting A classical or Neoclassical design used on furniture and pilasters since the 16th century. It consists of parallel, usually vertical, concave grooves.

fret pattern See **key pattern.**

fretwork A form of decoration used on woodwork, especially with **chinoiserie,** of interlaced geometric designs carved into thin wood. Blind fretwork has a backing often of a contrasting wood or colour, whereas open fretwork does not.

frieze A decorative horizontal band at or above cornice height.

gasolier A gas light in the shape of a chandelier with glass shades. Usually made of brass and popular in the mid-19th century.

gate-leg table A form of extending table popular since the 17th century, which has rounded, hinged flaps. When lifted the flaps are supported by legs, or gates, which swing out from the centre of the table.

girandole An ornate candelabrum, usually in Rococo or Neoclassical style. The term also applies to elaborately carved or gilded **sconces** with reflecting mirrors.

gloss paint Oil-based paint with a shiny finish. It is used mainly for woodwork and metalwork.

graining A method of creating the appearance of wood with

paint. It is sometimes used to make cheap wood look like a superior one, such as walnut, but was also used as a decorative finish on panelling, in the 19th century.

guilloche A continuous figure-of-eight motif popular as a form of furniture decoration from the 16th century.

highboy Produced in North America from about 1700, this is a tall chest consisting of a chest of drawers set on a **lowboy** or **commode.** It was usually designed with a broken-arch pediment and **cabriole legs.**

hoof foot The end of a leg in the shape of a goat's hoof. Found on some early 18th-century and Queen Anne furniture.

inlay A decorative technique which involves inserting small pieces of ivory, metal, mother-of-pearl or different coloured woods into recesses carved into a wooden surface to create an image or design.

intarsia Elaborate form of pictorial **marquetry,** used on Renaissance and 16th-century German furniture.

iridescent glass The term originally described the prismatic appearance of ancient glass uncovered by archaeologists – this is caused by carbonic acid in the soil breaking up the surface. Following archaeological finds in the Near East in the 1870's glassworkers such as Tiffany started recreating this look by coating coloured glass with metallic oxides. (See **Favrile glass.**) It was also made in Austria, England and France from the 1870s.

Japan furniture A style popular in the West in the late 19th century characterized by spindly forms, **fretwork** in metal and wood, and **lacquerwork.**

japanning A technique of varnishing used in the West from the 1660s to emulate the **lacquerwork** of the Far East. It involved applying layers of heat-hardened spirit-based varnishes; later, oil-based varnishes were used.

jardinière A pedestal which supports a potted plant or on which flowers are placed.

kelim This flat-woven Middle-Eastern type of rug was originally made by nomads for their own use and typically has striking geometric patterns in bold colours.

key pattern A repeated design, also known as fret pattern, of straight lines at right angles, creating a maze-like effect. It originated from classical Greek architecture and is often used as a border.

Kidderminster A type of carpet made at Kidderminster, Worcestershire, from the early 17th century. Originally they were cheap floorcoverings but from the 18th century they were made from heavy wool combined with linen.

kneehole desk A desk with a space through the middle of it to allow a person's knees to be accommodated comfortably when sitting at the desk; i.e. it does not have a hinged worktop.

lacquerwork A high-gloss finish which originated in the Far East and which became very popular in Europe in the 17th century. Lacquer comes from the lacquer tree *Rhus vernicifera.*

ladderback chair A tall-backed chair with several narrow horizontal slats between the posts. A style adopted by Chippendale and other cabinetmakers of the 18th century.

lambrequin Lace decoration in the form of a short swag often used over the top of a door, window or mantelpiece, or a carved motif which imitates a lacy pattern. Also refers to lacy designs on porcelain.

latex paint See **emulsion paint.**

linenfold Woodwork carved to represent vertical folds of drapery. Popular in the 15th and 16th centuries on furniture and wall panelling, and during the 19th century Tudor Revival.

lit-en-bateau A distinctive bed with curving ends popular during the *Empire* period.

loo table A 19th century round **pedestal table** for playing the card game loo.

lowboy An American term for a form of dressing-table, usually with one long drawer and three short ones. Often made *en suite* with a **highboy**. The term is also used for English Queen Anne dressing-tables.

lunette Semicircular shape, often filled with carved ornament, used to decorate furniture during the 17th and 19th centuries.

lyre back The back of a chair in the form of lyre, which is roughly horseshoe-shaped with outwardly scrolled ends and with a horizontal bar between its arms. It was very popular in the late 18th century.

marbling A paint effect used from ancient Egyptian times to imitate polished marble.

marquetry A decorative **veneer** in which different pieces of wood or other materials form a pattern which is then applied to the surface of furniture.

matt paint Water or oil-based paint the finish of which shows little or no sheen.

medallion See **ceiling rose.**

Moorfields A design of hand-knotted carpet produced from the 1850s at Moorfields in London. Some of these were designed by Robert Adam.

mortise-and-tenon joint A joint used since the 16th century and made by inserting a projecting piece of wood, or tenon, into a hole, or mortise, cut into another piece of wood. The two might be secured by a dowel, or glued.

ogee-arch An arch formed by a concave and convex curve creating a serpentine shape identified with the Gothic style. It was used in neo-Gothic furniture on chair backs and wooden panelling as well as in architectural mouldings.

opaline glass Also called opal glass, this white or coloured (often green) glass was fashionable in the 19th century.

oriel windows Projecting windows in an upper storey, usually in the **solar.**

ormolu Gilt decoration, the name of which derives from the French term *or moulu* (ground gold). It is also known as bronze doré, or gilt bronze.

ottoman The term derives from the Ottoman dynasty and is applied to a richly upholstered bench. In the 19th century it referred more widely to any overstuffed seat, with or without a back, including a **pouffe.**

papier mâché A substance made from sand, chalk, size and paper

pulp which is moulded when wet and then left to dry, forming a hard material. It was moulded into furniture in 19th-century Europe and North America.

parquet flooring Wooden flooring in which wood stripes are laid in a geometric design.

patera A medallion design, sometimes with **fluting** leaves or flower petals, and carved, painted or inlaid into Neoclassical furniture.

paw foot A furniture leg ending in the shape of a paw. It was used in ancient Egypt, classical Greece and Rome and became popular again from the late 17th to the 19th centuries.

pedestal table A table with a central column, which ends in a wide base or foot.

pelmet A band of fabric across the top of a window enclosing the curtain rail or decorating the **tester** of a four-poster bed. Sometimes this is in the same fabric as the curtain and can also be scalloped or fringed. The term also refers to a box which may cover the curtain rail.

pietre dure Decorative technique which originated in Italy at the beginning of the 17th century and which uses semi-precious stones. If only one stone is used this is *pietra dura*. A cheaper form of this work, using highly polished imitation stones, is called *scagliola*.

pilaster A semicircular or flattened column used to decorate a façade rather than for any structural support.

pouffe A round, large, heavily stuffed cushion that serves as a seat, fashionable from the early 19th century.

récamier A **day-bed** with curved ends, in the Neoclassical style. It takes its name from the portrait of Mme Récamier by Jacques Louis David.

reeding An ornamental style of parallel, usually vertical, convex moulding. The opposite of **fluting,** it also derives from the decoration on classical columns.

refectory table A long table, often made from oak, and originally made for the refectory of a monastery; replicas became fashionable during the 19th-century Gothic Revival.

relief A form of decoration created by applying moulding to, carving into, or stamping a surface. High-relief (*haut-relief* or *alto relievo*) refers to prominent decoration, whereas low relief (*bas-relief* or *basso relievo*) is flatter.

repoussé Raised decoration on soft metals such as copper and silver, and made by hammering the metal from the back.

roundel Any circular ornament, such as a decorative medallion. See also **patera.**

Roycroft furniture American Arts and Crafts furniture produced by the Roycroft Community from 1896. Its designs were plain and were generally made from oak, ash or mahogany, often with copper fittings, prominent **mortise-and-tenon joints** and tapering legs.

rush-seating Rushes plaited to form a chair seat; common in Europe and America in the 18th and 19th centuries.

salt-glazed stoneware A form of ceramic, between earthenware and porcelain, which vitrifies at a very high temperature and which is glazed with ordinary salt, thrown into the kiln at the time of firing. It forms a transparent hard glaze, sometimes with a pitted effect. Often associated with the British Arts and Crafts movement.

Savonnerie carpet A highly decorative French carpet from a factory founded in the early 17th century, which was once a soap factory (hence 'savonnerie'). The designs were European but used some Eastern techniques, such as the Ghiordes knot. It merged with Gobelins in the early 19th century.

scagliola See *pietre dure.*

sconce A candle-holder or lamp mounted on a wall, with one or more holders. In the 18th century they were made in silver or brass.

secretaire (secretary) A desk with drawers concealed by a hinged flap which forms the writing surface. Dates from the 18th century.

semi-gloss paint See **eggshell paint.**

settle A plain, high-backed wooden seat with arms, for two or more people. Some have a hinged seat which covers a chest beneath it. Made from the 17th century onwards.

shagreen Usually, sharkskin, dyed green and used as a cover for 18th century sword handles, knife boxes, etc.

Shaker Furniture, metalwork and textiles produced by the Shaker community in North America from the late 18th century. It is characterized by a simple, functional appearance, tapering legs, swallow-tail joints, the use of local woods and immense care paid to small details and obvious construction.

shellwork A form of decoration which uses shells of various shapes and colours, mounted in metal as ornaments or vases, or applied to plaster on boxes or mirror frames. Sometimes combined with paper filigree.

skirting (baseboard) A border, usually of wood but sometimes of plaster, covering the base of a wall where it meets the floor.

solar A chamber on an upper floor, usually a parlour or withdrawing room.

strap-hinge A hinge with a long bar, or leaf, which reaches right across a door.

strapwork A design of interlocking strap-like bands, which originated in the Netherlands in the 16th century and which appeared on North European furniture from the 16th and 17th centuries. It became fashionable again in the 19th century.

stucco work Plaster or cement moulding used as a form of architectural decoration.

Sussex chair A type of chair produced in the 19th century by the firm of William Morris. It had a **lyre back** with spindles, a rush seat and **ebonized** wood.

swag See **festoon.**

tabouret A low, upholstered stool, made from the 17th century onwards.

tatami mat A straw mat, about 2 × 1m (6 × 3ft), commonly used as a floor covering in Japan from the 10th century onwards.

tea-table In the 18th century, any small occasional table that tea could be served from. It could have a detachable top, or unfold into a card table.

tester The flat canopy that joins the posts on a four-poster bed.

Thonet bentwood Bentwood was invented by the Austrian cabinetmaker Michael Thonet (1796-1871) and was mass-produced in cheap wood from the mid-19th century onwards.

ticking A strong linen or cotton fabric usually striped, used to cover mattresses and pillows, and for hanging in doorways.

tie-back A length of fabric, cord Or similar attached to a window-frame and used to loop back a curtain. This is also known as an *embrasse.*

Tiffany glass Stained-glass pendant lamps and table lamps. See also **Favrile glass** and **iridescent glass.**

tinderbox A box containing tinder, flint and steel with which a fire could be instantly kindled.

Trafalgar chair There were several objects designed in recognition of Nelson's victory, including two chair types: a Regency chair with a cane seat, curved legs and cable moulding along the crest rail and posts; and a Sheraton chair decorated with nautical symbols such as dolphins and anchors.

travertine A white or pale-coloured rock, used by Mies van der Rohe and other followers of the International Style.

trefoil A Gothic motif in the form of 3 symmetrical lobes, rather like a clover leaf; a quatrefoil has 4 leaves. Used in furniture in the Gothic Revival of the 19th century.

trophy A decorative design carved in **relief** in wood, usually a composition of arms and banners, musical instruments, or other related objects. Popular in the Rococo period. See also *boiserie.*

valance A horizontal strip of fabric fixed over a window or canopy, or the equivalent element in wood, such as the horizontal board under the surface of a table.

veneer A very thin layer of wood, usually a valuable one such as mahogany, rosewood or walnut, which is glued to the surface of a piece of furniture of inferior wood. It is also sometimes used to disguise construction details.

Vernis Martin A **lacquer** or **japanning** technique which typically produced a dark green colour and which was invented in France *c.*1730 by the Martin brothers. However, it was used to produce other colours too.

vitrine A display cabinet with a glass front, free-standing or placed on a stand, usually made in the 19th century.

volute An ornamental form of spiral scroll used on furniture, adopted from Ionic capitals in Greek architecture.

wainscoting An additional surface, usually of wood, applied to the lower part of an interior wall. See **dado.**

whatnot A small open cabinet for displaying objects, often with small drawers below the open shelves. Popular from the Regency period onwards. See also *étagère.*

Wilton A **Brussels**-type carpet with a velvety appearance created by the cut loops of the pile. These were made in Wiltshire from the first half of the 18th century.

Windsor chair A type of chair produced in large quantities in Britian from the late 17th century and popular from the mid-18th. It was fashionable too in North America. It had turned legs, stretchers and spindles, a curved back saddle seat and splayed legs.

work-table Usually a lady's sewing-table, small, square or oval-shaped, with a hinged top that contained compartments for needlework. It often had a bag or pouch suspended beneath it.

INDEX

INDEX

INDEX

ACKNOWLEDGEMENTS

DEDICATION

For Leila Stone who cares for old houses as much as I do

AUTHOR'S ACKNOWLEDGEMENTS

I have many people to thank for help with this book. I am grateful for the kindness of those who let their houses be photographed, particularly Mr and Mrs John B. Schorsch and Mr and Mrs Josef Bauer. I dread to think what my life would be like without the immense help and loyal support of my assistant Abigael Sullivan. And, of course, nothing could have been produced without the dedication and liveliness of mind of Pippa Lewis and Jessica Walton, who did the picture research. Meryl Lloyd, the Art editor of the project, Alison Shackleton and Ruth Prentice who designed it, and Debora Robertson and Jane Harcus who worked so hard on getting so much of the contents together. My patient, tactful and inspiring editor Polly Powell, made the whole project a pleasure to undertake and I have always to thank Alison Cathie, Ray Roberts and Felicity Bryan for their constant support and enthusiasm, as well as my colleagues Jim Heineman and Ken Stenger.

PICTURE CREDITS

1 National Trust Photographic Library/Michael Boys; 2 Bradford City Art Gallery/Bridgeman Art Library; 6 Paul G.Beswick; 7 *above* World Press Network/ Trevor Richards; 7 *below left* Richard Bryant/Arcaid; 7 *below right* Lars Hallen; 8-9 Simon Brown/ Conran Octopus; 10-11 Sotheby's, London; 12 National Trust Photographic Library/Mike Williams; 13 Richard Bryant/Arcaid; 14 Lucinda Lambton/Arcaid; 15 *above* Musée Cluny, Paris/Bridgeman Art Library/ Giraudon; 15 *below left* National Trust Photographic Library/C.Newsholme; 15 *below right* A.F.Kersting; 16 National Trust Photographic Library/ Mike Williams; 17 *above* C.S.Sykes; 17 *below* Guy Bouchet; 19 Derry Moore; 20 *left* C.S.Sykes; 20 *right* Fritz von der Schulenburg; 21 Edifice/Gillian Darley; 23 Agence Top/Basnier; 24 Fritz von der Schulenburg; 25 *above* A.F.Kersting; 25 *centre* Derry Moore; 25 *below* Peter Baistow; 26 Lucinda Lambton/Arcaid; 27 The National Gallery, London; 28 Ianthe Ruthven; 29 *above* Giraudon; 29 *below left* Bastin & Evrard; 29 *below right* Andreas Eisindael/ Elizabeth Whiting & Associates; 30-1 Bastin & Evrard; 32 J.F.Jaussaud/Stylograph; 33 Giraudon; 34 *above* Guy Bouchet; 34 *below* Edifice/Gillian Darley; 35 Lars Hallen; 36 *above* Angelo Hornak/RIBA; 36 *centre* E.T.Archive (Private Collection); 36 *below* Edifice/ Gillian Darley; 37 National Trust Photographic Library; 38 J.F.Jaussaud/Stylograph; 39 Derry Moore; 40 Sir John Soane Museum/Bridgeman Art Library; 41 Fritz von der Schulenburg; 42 *left* Paul G. Beswick; 42 *right* Richard Bryant/Arcaid; 43 Paul G. Beswick; 44-5 C.S.Sykes; 45 *right* Peter Baistow; 46 *above* Stoelite/Stylograph; 46 *centre* Ianthe Ruthven; 46 *below* Fritz von der Schulenburg; 47 *right* C.S.Sykes; 47 *left* National Trust Photographic Library/Susan Witney; 49 *left* National Trust Photographic Library/Tim Stephens; 49 *centre* Derry Moore; 49 *right* National Trust Photographic Library/ Richard Surman; 50 Lucinda Lambton/Arcaid; 51 Derry Moore; 54 C.S.Sykes; 56-7 Richard Bryant/Arcaid; 57 *right* Paul G. Beswick; 58 Richard Bryant/Arcaid; 59 *left* Richard Bryant/Arcaid; 59 *right* Paul G. Beswick; 62 Fritz von der Schulenburg; 63 *above* Giraudon/ Lauros; 63 *below left* Musée des Arts Decoratifs, Paris; 63 *below right* Fritz von der Schulenburg; 64 Giraudon/Lauros; 65 *left* Gilles de Chabaneix/ Stylograph; 65 *right* Agence Top/Catherine Bibollet; 66-7 Lars Hallen; 68 *above* Fritz von der Schulenburg; 68 *below* A.F.Kersting; 69 Richard Bryant/Arcaid; 70 Angelo Hornak/British Museum; 71 *above* Derry Moore; 71 *below* Angelo Hornak; 72 Angelo Hornak; 73 Giraudon/Lauros; 74-5 National Trust Photographic Library/John Bethell; 75 *right* Fritz von der Schulenburg; 76 Gilles de Chabaneix/ Stylograph; 78 Richard Paul/Stylograph; 79 Lars Hallen; 82 Guy Bouchet; 83 *above* Guy Bouchet; 83 *below* Gilles de Chabaneix/Stylograph; 84-5 Lucinda Lambton/Arcaid; 85 *right* C.S.Sykes; 86 House &

Interiors; 87 *left* Ianthe Ruthven; 87 *right* Lucinda Lambton/Arcaid; 88 National Trust Photographic Library/Nick Carter; 89 Lucinda Lambton/Arcaid; 92 *left* Karl Dietrich-Buhler/Elizabeth Whiting and Associates; 92 *centre* Peter Woloszynski/Elizabeth Whiting and Associates; 92 *right* Peter Woloszynski; 93 National Trust Photographic Library/Nick Carter; 94-5 Angelo Hornak; 95 *right* Derry Moore; 96 Richard Bryant/Arcaid; 97 *left* Angelo Hornak; 97 *right* Derry Moore; 101 Angelo Hornak; 102-3 John Hall; 104 Anthony Paine (Parker Hobart); 105-6 John Hall; 108 Martin Trelwaney; 109 *above* Giraudon/ Lauros; 109 *below left* Richard Bryant/Arcaid; 109 *below right* House & Interiors; 110 *above* Greg Hursley; 110 *below* Edifice/Gillian Darley; 111 Christie's, London/Bridgeman Art Library; 112 World of Interiors/James Mortimer; 113 Bastin & Evrard; 114 *above* Martin Trelawny; 114 *centre left* National Trust Photographic Library/John Bethell; 114 *centre right* J.F.Jaussaud/Stylograph; 115 Christie's Colour Library; 116 Courtesy of Hazlitt, Goodon & Fox, London; 117 Lars Hallen; 118 *left* World of Interiors/James Mortimer; 118 *right* Greg Hursley; 119 Fritz von der Schulenburg; 120 Richard Bryant/Arcaid; 121 *left* National Trust Photographic Library/J. Pirkin; 121 *above right* Marianne Haas/ Stylograph; 121 *below right* Derry Moore; 122-3 National Trust Photographic Library/Graham Challifour; 123 *right* Richard Bryant/Arcaid; 124 *left* Jerry Tubby/Elizabeth Whiting and Associates; 124 *right* Country Life/Tim Imrie; 125 Derry Moore; 126 *above* Lucinda Lambton/Arcaid; 126 *below* Richard Bryant/Arcaid; 127 *above* Derry Moore; 130 Derry Moore; 132-3 Ianthe Ruthven; 133 *right* National Trust Photographic Library/Michael Boys; 135 *below* Greg Hursley; 135 *above right* House & Interiors; 136 Greg Hursley; 137 *Lars* Hallen; 140 Marianne Haas/Stylograph; 141 Neil Lorimer/Elizabeth Whiting and Associates; 143 *above* Paul Ryan/J.B.Visual Press; 143 *below left* Derry Moore; 143 *below right* Michael Holford; 144 *above* Cheltenham Art Gallery & Museums/Bridgeman Art Library; 144 *below* Lucinda Lambton/Arcaid; 145 E.T.Archive (Museum der Stadt Wieni, Vienna); 146 Richard Bryant/Arcaid; 148 *above* Tim Street-Porter/Elizabeth Whiting and Associates; 148 *below* Edifice/Pippa Lewis; 149 Balthazar Korab; 150 *left* Guy Bouchet; 150 *centre* Spike Powell/Elizabeth Whiting and Associates; 150 *right* Rainsville Archive; 151 Edimedia/Jacqueline Guillot (Connaissance des Arts); 152 *above* Ianthe Ruthven; 152 *below* Ianthe Ruthven; 153 Victoria and Albert Museum/Bridgeman Art Library; 154-5 Richard Bryant/Arcaid; 156 *above* Tim Street-Porter/ Elizabeth Whiting and Associates; 157 *above left* Derry Moore; 157 *right* Balthazar Korab; 158 *left* National Trust Photographic Library/J.Gibson; 158 *above right* Tim Street-Porter/Elizabeth Whiting and Associates; 158 *below right* Derry Moore; 159 Balthazar Korab; 162 Derry Moore; 163 *above* Richard Bryant/Arcaid; 163 *below* Balthazar Korab;

164-5 Dennis Krukowski/Conran Octopus; 165 *right* Bastin & Evrard; 166 *left* Dennis Krukowski/Conran Octopus; 166 *right* Ianthe Ruthven; 167 *above* A.F.Kersting; 167 *below* Bastin & Evrard; 168 *left* Dennis Krukowski/Conran Octopus; 168 *right* Fritz von der Schulenburg; 172 *above* Ianthe Ruthven; 172 *below* Guy Bouchet; 173 La Maison de Marie Claire/ Hussenot/Belmont; 174-5 Spike Powell/Elizabeth Whiting and Associates; 175 *right* Paul Ryan/J.B.Visual Press; 176 *above* Paul Ryan/J.B.Visual Press; 176 *below* Ianthe Ruthven; 177 Derry Moore; 178 Lucinda Lambton/Arcaid; 179 Neil Lorimer/Elizabeth Whiting and Associates; 182 *above* Simon Brown/ Conran Octopus; 182 *below* Richard Bryant/Arcaid; 183 Simon Brown/Conran Octopus; 184 Camera Press; 185 *above* Angelo Hornak; 185 *below left* Richard Bryant/Arcaid; *below right* Mike Nicholson/ Elizabeth Whiting and Associates; 186 Bildarchiv Preussischer Kulturbesitz; 187 Paul Ryan/J.B.Visual Press; 188 Victoria and Albert Museum, London/ Bridgeman Art Library; 189 *above* Balthazar Korab; 189 *below left* Tim Street-Porter/Elizabeth Whiting and Associates; 189 *below right* Richard Bryant/ Arcaid; 190 Architectural Association/R.B.Vickery; 191 *above* Mike Nicholson/Elizabeth Whiting and Associates; 191 *below* Edifice/Pippa Lewis; 192 Dugied Mille/Stylograph; 193 *left* Dugied Mille/ Stylograph; 193 *right* Fritz von der Schulenburg; 194 E.T.Archive; 195 *below right* La Maison Française/ Christian Gervais; 196 Derry Moore; 197 Robert Opie; 198-9 Derry Moore; 199 *right* Richard Bryant/ Arcaid; 200 Stylograph; 201 *above* Richard Bryant/ Arcaid; 201 *below* Fritz von der Schulenburg; 202 *left* Richard Bryant/Arcaid; 202 *right* Fritz von der Schulenburg; 203 La Maison de Marie Claire/Rozes/ Hirsch Marie; 204 Simon Brown/Conran Octopus; 205 *above* Fritz von der Schulenburg; 205 *below* Derry Moore; 206-7 Simon Brown/Conran Octopus; 209 *left* La Maison de Marie Claire/Scotto/Belmont; 209 *right* La Maison de Marie Claire/Hussenot/Belmont; 210 Spike Powell/Elizabeth Whiting and Associates; 211 *above left* Ken Kirkwood; 211 *above left* E.T.Archive; 211 *below* Christie's Colour Library; 214-6 Ken Kirwood.

The following photographs were specially taken for Conran Octopus by:

Dennis Krukowski: Interior designed by Joan Arden Schorsch 100; Josef A.Bauer (designer Alex Fradkoff, New York) 195 *left*, 195 *above right*, 208; Trevor Richards: Little Holland House 142, 147, 156 *below*, 157 *below left*; Courtesy of the Heritage Service, London Borough of Sutton.

The following fabric and wallpaper photographs were specially taken for Conran Octopus by Ian Kalinowski and styled by Claire Lloyd 52-3, 61, 90-1, 98-9, 107, 128-9, 138-9, 162-3, 170-1, 180-1, 212-3

223

FABRIC AND WALLPAPER CREDITS

Many of the companies listed here are manufacturers or trade suppliers. Please telephone or write for stockists in your area.

1 GEORGIAN pages 52-53

1 MF4991.2 Monkwell Fabrics Ltd, 10-12 Wharfdale Road, Bournemouth, Dorset BH4 9BT, 0202-762 456; **2** From a selection at Rupert Cavendish Antiques, 610 King's Rd, London SW6 2DX, 01-731 7041; **3** From a selection at McKinney Kidston, 1 Wandon Rd, New King's Rd, London SW6 2GF, 01-384 1377; **4** Bedford Stripe ref 301 Hamilton Weston Wallpapers Ltd, 18 St Mary's Grove, Richmond, Surrey TW9 1UY, 01-940 4850; **5** Daisy/Original Zoffany Ltd, 63 South Audley St, London W1Y 5BF, 01-629 9262; **6** From a selection at Henry Newbery, 18 Newman St, London W1P 4AB, 01-636 2053; **7** From a selection at Henry Newbery (see **1.6**); **8** From a selection at The Gallery of Antique Costume & Textiles, 2 Church St, London NW8 8ED, 01-723 9981; **9** François Joseph 9819.96 Nobilis Fontan, 1&2 Cedar Studios, 45 Glebe Pl, London SW3 5JE, 01-352 3870; **10** MF4994.3 Monkwell Fabrics Ltd (see**1.1**); **11** From a selection at the Gallery of Antique Costume & Textiles (see **1.7**); **12** See **1**; **13** Bloomsbury Square ref 507, Hamilton Weston Wallpapers Ltd (see **1.4**); **14** BD33 Hamilton Weston Wallpapers Ltd (see **1.4**).

2 COLONIAL pages 60-61

1 From a selection at The London Architectural Salvage & Supply Co. Ltd (LASSCo), Mark St, London EC2A 4ER, 01-739 0448; **2** Gilmore 1375-153 Jab International Furnishings, 15-19 Cavendish Pl, London W1M 9DL, 01-636 1343; **3** Pallu & Lake, 1 Cringle St, London SW8 5BX, 01-627 5566; **4** Ticking 740 The Conran Shop, Michelin House, 81 Fulham Road, London SW3 6RD, 01-589 7401; **5** From a selection at Henry Newbery, 18 Newman St, London W1P 4AB, 01-636 2053; **6** Sudbury Park 7046/03 Colefax & Fowler, 39 Brook St, London W1Y 2JE, 01-493 2231; **7** Georgian Button 12-105 Cole & Son, 18 Mortimer St, London W1A 4BU, 01-580 2288; **8** Amity Check 805146 Lee Jofa at Pallu & Lake, (see **2.3**); **9** Gilmore 1375-146 Jab International Furnishings (see **2.2**); **10** Reichenhall 2124-139 Jab International Furnishings (see **2.2**); **11** Green Park ref 20 Hamilton Weston Wallpapers Ltd, 18 St Mary's Grove, Richmond, Surrey TW9 1UY, 01-940 4850; **12** Rose des vents 4051.901 Manuel Canovas, 2 North Terrace, Brompton Rd, London SW3 2BA, 01-225 2298; **13** Cadiz 2069-110 Jab International Furnishings (see **2.2**); **14** Bankura 7977-199 Pallu & Lake (see **2.3**); **15** Gilmore 1375-260 Jab International Furnishings (see **2.2**).

3 EMPIRE pages 80-81

1 Rayure Tallieu 4103 HA Percheron, 97-99 Cleveland St, London W1P 5PN, 01-580 5156; **2 & 3** From a selection at Rupert Cavendish Antiques, 610 King's Rd, London SW6 2DX, 01-731 7041; **4** Damas Empire 13607 HA Percheron (see **3.1**); **5** Recamier borders FB233, CB109, CB105 & CB106 Cole & Son, 18 Mortimer St, London W1A 4BU, 01-580 2288; **6** Damas Corday 130/6 HA Percheron (see **3.1**); **7 & 8** From a selection at Distinctive Trimmings, 17d Kensington Church St, London W8, 01-937 6174; **9** Malmaison 9446/76 HA Percheron (see **3.1**); **10** Malmaison 9446/56 Henry Newbery, 18 Newman St, London W1P 4AB, 01-636 2053; **11** Lampas Les Abeilles 4023/03 HA Percheron (see **3.1**); **12** Red drag Alexander Beauchamp, Griffin Mill, Thrupp, Nr. Stroud, Gloucestershire GL5 2AZ, 0453-884537; **13** Galon greque 9093 Pierre Frey, 1 Cringle St, London SW8 5BX, 01-978 1291; **14** Windsor Stripe 13/SR-546 Cole & Son (see **3.5**).

4 REGENCY pages 90-91

1 From a selection at McKinney Kidston, 1 Wandon Rd, New King's Rd, London SW6 2GF, 01-384 1377; **2** From a selection at Rupert Cavendish Antiques, 610 King's Rd, London SW6 2DX, 01-731 7041; **3** Corinne GP63051, Warner Fabrics PLC, 7-11 Noel St, London W1V 4AL, 01-439 2411; **4** Rupert Cavendish Antiques (see **4.1**); **6** Kingston Market 8131 Hamilton Weston Wallpapers Ltd, 18 St Mary's Grove, Richmond, Surrey TW9 1UY, 01-940 4850; **7** Carnation/Original Zoffany Ltd, 63 South Audley St, London W1Y 5BF, 01-629 9262; **8** From a selection at the Gallery of Antique Costume & Textiles, 2 Church St, London NW8 8ED, 01-723 9581; **9** Monkwell Fabrics Ltd, 10-12 Wharfdale Road, Bournemouth, Dorset BH4 9BT, 0202-762 456; **10** From a selection at McKinney Kidston (see **4.1**); **11** From a selection at Pillows of London, 48 Church Street, London NW8 8ED, 01-723 3171; **12** Blickling Stripe A1132-01 GP & J Baker, 8 Berners Street, London W1P 4JA, 01-636 8412.

5 FEDERAL pages 98-99

1 Beauchamp GP61828 Warner Fabrics PLC 7-11 Noel St, London W1V 4AL, 01-439 2411; **2 & 3** From a selection at McKinney Kidston, 1 Wandon Rd, New King's Rd, London SW6 2GF, 01-384 1377; **4** Audley GP63295 Warner Fabrics PLC (see **5.1**); **5** Fancy Stripe CS 4361, Warner Fabrics PLC (see **5.1**); **6** Charlotte 50-1206/3 Elizabeth Eaton, 25a Basil St, London SW3 1BB, 01-589 0118; **7** Parsley 50-1203/3 Elizabeth Eaton (see **5.6**); **8** Longueville 1338D HA Percheron, 97-99 Cleveland St, W1P 5PN, 01-580 5156; **9** 684.646-5 Ian Mankin, 109 Regents Park Rd, London NW1 8UR, 01-722 0997; **10** From a selection at McKinney Kidston (see **5.2 & 3**).

6 BIEDERMEIER pages 106-107

1 From a selection at Henry Newbery, 18 Newman St, London W1P 4AB, 01-636 2053; **2** From a selection at Pierre Frey, 1 Cringle St, London SW8 5BX, 01-978 1291; **3** Riccione 2001-261 Jab International Furnishings, 15-19 Cavendish Pl, London W1M 9DL, 01-636 1343; **4** From a selection at Rupert Cavendish Antiques, 610 King's Rd, London SW6 2DX, 01-731 7041; **5** Ravenna 2171-155 Jab International Furnishings (see **6.3**); **6, 7 & 8** From a selection at Rupert Cavendish Antiques (see **6.4**); **9** El Moiree-sauvage C/30 St Leger Fabrics, Unit M15, Chelsea Garden Market, Chelsea Harbour, London SW10, 01-823 3789; **10** Piacenza 6169-249, Jab International Furnishings (see **6.3**); **11** Marsala 2888-113 Jab International Furnishings (see **6.3**); **12** From a selection at Henry Newbery (see **6.1**); **13** Celano 2891-117 Jab International Furnishings Ltd (see **6.3**); **14** Modena 222556 Jab International Furnishings (see **6.3**); **15** From a selection at Henry Newbery (see **6.1**); **16** Nota 624-506-4 Alton-Brooke, 5 Sleaford St, London SW8, 01-622 9372.

7 ECLECTICISM pages 128-129

1 From a selection at McKinney Kidston 1 Wandon Rd, New King's Rd, London SW6 2GF, 01-384 1377; **2** Acanthus scrolls GP62914 Warner Fabrics PLC, 7-11 Noel St, London W1V 4AL, 01-439 2411; **3** 'Holbein' Watts of Westminster, 7 Tufton St, London SW1P 3QE, 01-222 2893; **4** Minster EHC14 Mary Gilliatt's Indian Garden Collection, Turner Wallcoverings, 68/82 Brewery Road, London N7 9NE, 01-609 4201; **5** Forest Plaid, Pallu & Lake, 1 Cringle St, London SW8 5BX, 01-627 5566; **6** 'Oscar' Watts of Westminster (see **7.3**); **7** From a selection at The Gallery of Antique Costume & Textiles, 2 Church St, London MW8 8ED, 01-723 9981; **8** François Joseph 9819.92, Nobilis Fontan, 1&2 Cedar Studios, 45 Glebe Pl, London SW3 5JE, 01-352 3870; **9** From a selection at The Gallery of Antique Costume & Textiles (see **7.7**); **10 & 11** Vladimir 9865.93/9865.98 Nobilis Fontan (see **7.8**); **12** Maximilien 9795.92 Nobilis Fontan (see **7.8**); **13** From a selection at Pillows of London, 48 Church Street, London NW8 8ED, 01-723 3171; **14** El Moiree-Sauvage C/10 St Leger Fabrics, Unit M15, Chelsea Graden Market, London SW10, 01/823 3789.

8 HIGH VICTORIAN pages 138-139

1 Sari FR1 R1237 GP & J Baker, 8 Berners St, London W1, 01-636 8412; **2** From a selection at The Gallery of Antique Costumes & Textiles, 2 Church St, London NW8 8ED, 01-723 9981; **3** From a selection at Pillows of London, 48 Church St, London NW8 8ED, 01-723 3171; **4** Indian Fuchsia 10911/01 Colefax & Fowler, 39 Brook St, London W1Y 2JE, 01-493 2231; **5** Kashmir Trellis CS5763 Warner Fabrics PLC 7-11 Noel St, London W1V 4AL, 01-493 2411; **6** Anaglypta Supadurable RD148, Crown Decorative Products Ltd, Hollins Rd, Darwen, Lancashire; **7** Kashmir border BEY 1383 Warner Fabrics PLC (see **8.5**); **8** Blackberry CHE.06 Zoffany Ltd, 63 South Audley St, London W1Y 5BF, 01-629 9262; **9** Small vine OEW-150 Cole & Son, 18 Mortimer St, London W1A 4BU, 01-580 2288; **10** Dahlia Garden CS5850 Warner Fabrics PLC (see **8.5**); **11** From a selection at The Gallery of Antique Costumes & Textiles (see **8.2**); **12** From a selection at McKinney Kidston, New King's Rd, London SW6 2GF, 01-384 1377; **13** From a selection at Lunn Antiques Ltd, 86 New King's Rd, London SW6, 01-736 4638.

9 ARTS AND CRAFTS pages 160-161

1 'Wyvern' Watts of Westminster, 7 Tufton St, London SW1P 3QE, 01-222 2893; **2** Acorn PR7422 Sanderson & Sons, 52 Berners St, London W1, 01-636 7800; **3** From a selection at The London Architectural Salvage & Supply Co Ltd (LASSCo), Mark St, London EC2A 4ER, 01-739 0448; **4** From a selection at The Gallery of Antique Costume & Textiles, 2 Church St, London NW8 8ED, 01-723 9981; **5** Harvest (green) The Habitat V&A Collection, Habitat, 196 Tottenham Court Road, London W1A, 01-631 3880; **6** Farfalla's Lace GP62955 Warner Fabrics PLC, 7-11 Noel St, London W1V 4AL, 01-439 2411; **7** 'Nimue', Watts of Westminster (see **9.1**); **8** Willow Sanderson & Sons (see **9.2**); **9** 'Clarence' Watts of Westminster (see **9.1**); **10** Acanthus PR7391/2, Sanderson & Sons (see **9.2**); **11** Harvest (rust) The Habitat V&A Collection (see **9.5**).

10 ART NOUVEAU pages 170-171

1 From a selection at Westland Pilkington, The Clergy House, Mark St, London EC2A 4ER, 01-739 8094; **2** Hera Liberty Retail Limited, Regent St, London W1R 6AH, 01-734 1234; **3** Ianthe Liberty Retail Limited (see **10.2**); **4** Tea rose Alexander Beauchamp, Griffin Mill, Thrupp, Nr. Stroud, Gloucestershire GL5 2AZ, 0453-884537; **5** Magnolia Alexander Beauchamp (see **10.4**); **6** From a selection at The London Architectural Salvage & Supply Co. Ltd. (LASSCo), Mark St, London EC2A 4ER, 01-739 0448; **7** Corn Alexander Beauchamp (see **10.4**).

11 EDWARDIAN pages 180-181

1 Fancy Stripe CS4360 Rose Warner Fabrics PLC, 7-11 Noel St, London W1V 4AL, 01-636 1343; **2** Border Designers Guild, 271 & 277 King's Rd, London W12 7SJ, 01-351 5775; **3** Riccione 2001-154 Jab International Furnishings, 15-19 Cavendish Place, London W1M 9DL, 01-636 1343; **4** From selection at Henry Newbery, 18 Newman St, London W1P 4AB, 02-636 2053; **5** Border CB133, Cole & Son, 18 Mortimer St, London W1A 4BU, 01-580 2288; **6** Rosedale 1480/01 Colefax & Fowler, 39 Brook St, London W1Y 2JE, 01-493 2231; **7** Chambrey 8581-167 Jab International Furnishings (see **10.3**); **8** From a selection at The Gallery of Antique Costume & Textiles, 2 Church St, London NW8 8ED, 01-723 9981; **9** Pastoral chintz CMS56236 Lee Jofa at Warner Fabrics PLC (see **11.1**); **10** From a selection at Henry Newbery (see **11.4**); **11** Wallpaper Georgian stripe Warner Fabrics PLC (see **11.1**); **12** Cote Jardin WC1 36044 Nobilis Fontan, 1&2 Cedar Studios, 45 Glebe Pl, London SW3 5JE; **13** Cote Jardin WC1 36033 Nobilis Fontan (see **11.12**).

12 ART DECO pages 212-213

1 Stainless steel – photographer's own **2** Cyrenaika 2354-181 Jab International Furnishings, 15-19 Cavendish Pl, London W1M 9DL, 01-636 1343 **3** Quadro 11-6064-150 Intair at Mary Fox Linton, 249 Fulham Rd, SW3 6HY, 01-351 0273 **4** Jab International Furnishings (see **12.2**) **5** Rennie 091, The Conran Shop, Michelin House, 81 Fulham Rd, London SW3 6RD, 01-589 7401 **6** America 2 543229 Nobilis Fontan, 1&2 Cedar Studios, 45 Glebe Pl, London SW3 5JE, 01-352 3870 **7** Ballina 4169 Manuel Canovas Ltd, 2 North Terrace, Brompton Rd, London SW3 2BA, 01-225 2298 **8** Leopardo 6346-01 HA Percheron, 97/99 Cleveland St, London W1, 01-580 5156 **9** From a selection at The London Architectural Salvage & Supply Co (LASSCo), Mark St, London EC2A 4ER, 01-739 0448 **10** Jim Thompson Designs PMS-2573B, Mary Fox Linton (see **12.3**) **11** Mure 2406-189 Jab International Furnishings (see **12.2**) **12** Dino 2451-193 Jab International Furnishings (see **12.2**).